ALL YOU WANTED TO KNOW ABOUT LOVE, BUT REFUSED TO ACCEPT

J. E. WHITE

WESTBOW
PRESS
A DIVISION OF THOMAS NELSON

WestBow Press books may be ordered through booksellers or by contacting:

WestBow Press
A Division of Thomas Nelson
1663 Liberty Drive
Bloomington, IN 47403
www.westbowpress.com
1 (866) 928-1240

Scripture taken from the King James Version of the Bible.

ISBN: 978-1-4908-1696-8 (sc)
ISBN: 978-1-4908-1698-2 (hc)
ISBN: 978-1-4908-1697-5 (e)

Library of Congress Control Number: 2013921434

Printed in the United States of America.

WestBow Press rev. date: 12/03/2013

DEDICATION

This book is dedicated to all the women who have rejected, abused, slandered, manipulated, and betrayed me. Also, to all the guys whom I considered friends, but stabbed me in the back. Thank you for the lessons I learned. Without you, this book may not have been written.

CONTENTS

INTRODUCTION

This book is about love. I've taken on the task of writing this book because I believe in love, and love seems to be on the verge of becoming extinct. Of course, that will never happen, but I want to put in my two cents, so I can say I helped keep love alive.

It seems that sex has replaced love, and everyone who wants love is trying to meet that need through sex. That has never worked, and it will not work now. You can't obtain momentary pleasure, and expect that pleasure to evolve into everlasting joy.

People are afraid. They are reluctant, skeptical, and disappointed. They shy away from love, because they've been hurt. The reason people have been hurt is; they do not know what love is. They get into relationships thinking they've found love. When the truth is revealed, however, they discover that what they thought was love, was not love at all.

This book will define love for you. Not only will it help define love, this book will also help you recognize love. The traits and characteristics of love are in this book. This is not anything new. This is just information you refused to accept, in the past.

Marriage is out of style, now. Shacking is in! Is cohabitation more politically correct? Sorry! With shacking, you can leave the relationship anytime you want. It's really convenient, because there is no commitment. Isn't it strange how people are willing to share their genitals with each other, but are afraid to share their hearts? Now, to me, that's crazy.

People are suspicious, now. They do not trust anyone. They live in shells to protect themselves from hurt and deception. This book will enable you to ascertain true love. You will not have to live in a shell. You won't have to live in fear. When marriage comes up, you will know if you are marrying the right person. There will be no doubt about it! The information in this book will take uncertainty away.

I do not claim to know it all, when it comes to love. I am just a man who has had some experiences with love. Some were joyous. Some were not so joyous. Some were in the world, and some were in the church. Over all, I have learned a great deal through the things I have suffered. I thank God for allowing the Holy Spirit to make sense out of the things I have gone through.

Some things I did not understand, but the revelation of the Holy Spirit uncovered the mystery of what I did not understand. Now, I am sharing what he has given me, with you. I hope you enjoy reading this book. I do hope you will look at love differently, afterwards.

I refuse to believe that people, who have experienced disappointment in love, are satisfied. I believe they still want love in their lives. This book is written to help people like that. After reading this book, those who have been hurt, betrayed, and disappointed, will find new confidence in themselves, and in the capability of knowing true love.

The devil isn't going to like this book. This book is going to open too many eyes, and free too many people. The lies told about love are now exposed. The truth about love is now revealed. Do not reject it this time. Accept it!

All scripture references are from the King James Version, unless otherwise noted.

CHAPTER 1

WHERE DOES LOVE
COME FROM?

Most of the definitions of love are fabricated. Look around! Many people are living by made-up concepts that aren't true. They have no idea what love really is. They follow their feelings. If it feels right, then, it must have some validity to it. I know you've heard this conversation between the bride and the maid of honor. "Girl, are you sure this is the right guy for you?" asks the maid of honor. The bride replies, "Oh, I know it is. Everything just *feels* right." It may feel right, but do feelings provide the foundation for a true analysis? We know that's not true because of how relationships end. They don't last long. Somebody always gets hurt, deceived, manipulated, or betrayed. That's not a portrait of true love.

Other sources from which people get their definitions of love reside in their desires for what they want the love of their lives to be. Have you ever heard this? "Girl, he has to be good looking, financially secure, have his own home, educated, generous, and have no children. I don't have time to deal with two or three baby-mamas. You know they'll bring those kids to the house, and drop them off, to go party. They might come back and get them, and

1

they might not. Sometimes, they don't. Then, you're stuck with a family you didn't ask for. I want an honest man, who will love only me. I don't want a whoremonger." Sound familiar?

You later discover your dreamboat is honest because he uses it as a cover-up. He doesn't have any children because he doesn't want a family. He wants to live like a jet setter, having a prosperous career, partying all over the country. He wants to look eligible to other women, to be a man with no children, no wife, and the freedom to go when he pleases.

This book is going to set the record straight about love. You can discard all of the old concepts that have not worked in the past. This book marks the dawning of a new day. Your eyes will be opened, but you won't feel like you've never heard this before. You've already heard these truths. You just didn't accept them. Now, this incredible information is here again for you to reevaluate. Don't reject it this time.

Where Does Love Come From?

We may not know where love comes from just yet. We do know, however, that we haven't found it where we've already looked. So, let's look in a new place, the Word of God. No doubt, the answer is there. Let's examine the following passage of scripture.

> "Beloved, let us love one another: for love is of God; And every one that loveth is born of God, and knoweth God. He that loveth not, knoweth not God; for God is love." (1 John 4: 7-8)

John, the writer of the above scripture, is evidently talking to people of the household of faith. Church people! He's urging them to love one another, so others may see love coming from them. John wants them to show that *love is of God*, which means God is the source of love. Let's look further.

While people may want love, they must realize that to *seek love is to seek God*, because *love comes from God*. This means you can't find it. You must ask God for it. You must pray to contact the source of love. God's nature is love. His make-up is love. His character is love. His entire being is love. His judgment is love. His chastening is love, like when a father chastises his son. His grace is love. His mercy is love. Everything about God is love. If you ask him for it, he'll give it to you.

The mistake people make is that they seek the people they want, instead of seeking God. You know why? They believe that individuals are the source of the love they want. Of course, that's not true. No one is the source of love. They may be able to share love, or they may have love inside them, but they aren't the source of love. The source of love rests in a much higher place than we are. It's a more devine entity than we are. The only way anyone can reach that higher place is through prayer. Isn't that how we reach God—through prayer?

People look in all the wrong places, searching for love. Consequently, they're hurt, deceived, and mistreated. This happens because of the fabricated concepts they have of love. So many people create their own definition of love, and decide where they can find it. Of course, none of this information is valid, but that doesn't stop their quests for love, even if the paths they choose are the wrong paths.

My prayer is that whoever is reading this will accept what the word of God says: "Love is of God." Don't go to the strip club looking for love. Don't go to the casino, looking for love. Don't go to Motel 6, looking for love. Don't go to the racetrack. You want love in your life? Ask God to come into your life. He is the source of love. That's the part people have refused to accept. They want love, but they don't want God. Well, you can' have one, without the other.

One thing is for sure. If people are to experience love, they must be sure the people they want in their lives have love in them, too. You won't enjoy love just because you fancy someone, and feel you can't live without him or her. That person must possess love, in order to be able to give it. Let's look, again, into this scripture and see who has love, and who doesn't.

Who Is Capable Of Giving Love?

Now that we've established where love comes from, let's see what this scripture says about who you should seek out for a relationship. This is where fabricated theories may have to be dropped. Ladies and gentlemen, I know you have the type of mate you want in your mind already. I just want to let you know this: You may have to give up those ideas, if you want the one God has for you. Okay? Let's go a little deeper into this scripture, 1 John 4: 7-8.

The next thing this scripture says is this: "Everyone that loveth is born of God, and knoweth God."

It appears this scripture is pointing out who is capable of loving, and who isn't. It says plainly that those who love are the people "who are born of God." Now, I know most of you have heard of the born-again experience, which happens when a person gives his or her life to Jesus Christ. At that point, that person receives the Holy Spirit and becomes a new person, hence the term born-again. Watch this! When the newly reborn person receives the Holy Spirit, that spirit is love.

This scripture says that only those who have been born again are capable of loving, because they are the only people who have love *dwelling in them*. Not only are these people capable of giving,

4

receiving, and sharing love, they also *know* God. How do they know God? They have a relationship with him, through the power and intimacy of the Holy Spirit. Let's go a little further in our examination of this text.

This scripture may be disappointing to some people. They may not want to accept the fact that only the born-again individual possesses love. For instance, a lot of women like bad boys. We live in a society where the player's syndrome and the pimp syndrome are prevalent. Hustlers and rappers are what a lot of women like, today. All I have to say is this: you may get what you want, but you won't get love. If the person you are attracted to isn't saved, or born again, he doesn't have love to give. Remember! Everyone who loves is "born of God, and knows God."

You can' give something you don't have. If a person is not born of God, he or she doesn't have the capacity to love. Why? God hasn't given to them his spirit. They may be rich, cute, and have a lot of swagger. Without being born-again, however, they haven't been given the power of love, or the presence of love. Therefore, they don't have love to give. In the natural state, humanity cannot understand love because love is spiritual. A person, in their natural state, sees all spiritual things as foolishness.

Therefore, when you bring love up to the natural man, he thinks you are talking foolishness. He can't comprehend love, because love is too high for his finite mentality. Subsequently, he brings you down to his level, and begins to talk about sex. He understands sex. It's tangible. He can see it, and touch it. Spiritual things like love, however, are things the natural man just can't comprehend. Without the spirit of God inside of him, understanding spiritual things is impossible for him.

Ladies, don't be disappointed when the only way some men can relate to you is through sex. I am sure you have been through that before. You may have even found it necessary to tell a few men off for disrespecting you, in such a manner. Now, you know why they do it. Man, in his natural state can only refer to what he considers love to be, even if his concept is wrong and far-fetched. Look at what the Bible says about man in his natural state.

> "The natural man receiveth not the things of the spirit of God; for they are foolishness unto him: neither can he know them, because they are spiritually discerned." (1 Corinthians. 2: 14)

Those who haven't been born of God can't receive spiritual things. That includes love. As a matter of fact, spiritual things are foolishness to them. They are unable to understand love, because love is spiritually comprehended. The Holy Spirit must be inside you, in order for you to understand love. If you really want love, you must start looking at those who are saved. "Those who love are born of God, and know God."

Wait a minute! We aren't finished with this scripture in I John 4: 7, 8. We discussed who has the power to love, and who knows God. We also discovered that only those who have been born of God can love, and knows God. Now, let us go on to the latter part of this text, which says, "He that loveth not knoweth not God; for God is love."

We have briefly talked about man in his natural state, and how he can't love. Neither can he understand, ascertain, or comprehend love. The natural man doesn't know God, and doesn't have the power to decipher anything spiritually. There is no relationship, because there is no presence of God, in the natural man.

Man, in his natural state, can only give human affection. Some women settle for that, but it doesn't last long. Why? No one can love in his own power. The spiritual can't be implemented by human will or volition. The power to love comes from a higher source—God himself—because "God is love."

God Is Love, and Love Is God

The reason people can't find love is because love is invisible. The above scripture says God is love. I'm not going to have enough paper to really explain this topic, because it's so vast. I am, however, going to mention just enough for you to get a fair perspective of how these two entities match.

1. God is love. That means love is the same as God in character and essence.
2. God is a spirit. Love is the same spirit.
3. God never fails. Love never fails.
4. God is forever. Love is forever.
5. God is immutable, and changes not. Love is immutable, and changes not.
6. God never leaves you nor forsakes you. Love never leaves you nor forsakes you.
7. God came that you might have life and have it more abundantly. Love also seeks the highest good for the other person.
8. God gives. Love gives.
9. God sacrifices. Love sacrifices.
10. God takes the initiative to meet a need. Love takes the initiative to meet a need.

You can see that God and love are the same, and I haven't begun to touch the surface of this tremendous statement. I could go on and on. No one has love unless he or she is in God, and is born of God. To have God is to have love. Without God, there is no love. Without love, there is no spirit.

Let me give you another scripture that talks about God and love being the same, and if you don't have God, neither do you have love. Look at this scripture. It corroborates what I have said.

"And we have known and believed the love that
God hath to us. God is love; and he that dwelleth
in love, dwelleth in God, and God in him."
(1 John 4: 16)

I think the above scripture explains everything I have been
trying to say perfectly. "He that dwells in love, dwells in God,
and God in him." If you have one, you have the other. Now,
believe it or not, some people, even though they are now aware
of this, will still opt for a relationship where God is absent. Not
everyone wants God! Some people just want pleasure. They
want love without God, which is not going to happen. You
can't have love without God. You may think that what you
have is really love, even if neither of you is born of God. You
will discover you are wrong. God must be present, in order
for love to be present. That's it! That's all! Love and God are
synonymous.

You may say, "I know this couple who have been together for
thirty years. Neither of them ever went to church, and they love
each other. I know they do." Going to church is not what gives
you love. Love is the same as the Holy Spirit. The spirit is the life
of God, inside the believer. Whoever has that spirit has love, as
well as the presence of God. Both are the same, and he (the spirit)
is not given to people simply because they go to church. Read the
above scripture again, 1 John 4: 16.

The spirit of God doesn't enter a believer just because he or she
goes to church. There are a great number of people, in churches
across America, who don't have the Holy Spirit. They may have
been in church for years. Without the spirit of God, not only do
they not have the love of God, they're not saved, which means,
they are not even in the family of God.

The spirit of God comes into a person's life when a person
gives him or herself to Jesus Christ. That's when a person is born

again. The old person dies, and a new person emerges. Then, love lives inside that person. This can happen away from church, too. A person can receive Christ anywhere. Salvation doesn't have to take place at church. However, after a person is saved, he will join himself to a church that meets his spiritual needs, and helps him grow in the Lord.

There are many reasons people stay together. Some stay for sex, money, security. Who knows? Even without the spirit of God, people stay together. They stay for what they want, and for what they enjoy. They will say they are in love, and will really believe it. Even in the absence of God, people believe love is present. That's because they don't know God is love. Some people do know God is love, but they choose not to accept it, to enjoy what they like.

What have we talked about so far? We have shown where love originates. We talked about who is capable of giving and receiving love. Lastly, we talked about the main ingredient of love—the Spirit of God. We discovered that without God, love is not present. Now, let's talk about the people who try to deceive you, to make sure you know that the spirit in them is really the spirit of God. Read what the Word of God says you must do to protect yourself. How do you validate another spirit?

> "Beloved, believe not every spirit, but try the spirits whether they are of God: because many false prophets are gone out into the world. Hereby know ye the spirit of God: Every spirit that confesseth that Jesus Christ is come in the flesh is of God: And every spirit that confesseth not that Jesus Christ is come in the flesh is not of God: and this is that spirit of antichrist, whereof you have heard that it should come; and even now already is it in the world. (I John 4; 1-3)

The first thing this scripture says you must do is "Believe not every spirit, but try the spirits whether they are of God." This doesn't mean you must be suspicious of everyone. When, however, you see a red flag, it would be safer not to believe that spirit, until it can be validated as the spirit of God.

There will be times when you will attract people you are not attracted to. It's not your fault. You will encounter people who will try to deceive, manipulate, and hurt you. They will have a different spirit than you, a contrary spirit. Every word out of their mouths will be a lie, and the harder they try to impress you, the more ridiculous they will sound.

They know you are a believer, and that you love the Lord. They are also aware that you attend church regularly. In order for them to gain favor with you, they will lie and say they are saved, and they also go to church. The Bible says, "Try the spirits whether they are of God." How? Let us go a little deeper into the text, and see what *trying the spirits* actually means.

It appears that all you have to do is ask a question, or start a conversation about Jesus. The Bible says, "Every spirit that confesseth that Jesus Christ is come in the flesh is of God."

Not everyone believes in the virgin birth of Jesus. Many people claim they know God, but refuse to believe that Jesus actually came in the flesh, was born of a virgin, and lived on earth for 33 years. The Bible says that spirit is not of God, but is the spirit of the *antichrist* (1 John 4:3). Get away from that spirit! That spirit hates God, and everything related to God. He hates the church, the Word of God, and the people of God. He may try to fool you. Don't believe him! That spirit is not of God.

He hates holiness, and righteousness, because he hates doing what is right. He comes to steal, kill, and destroy. There is no love, no empathy, no sympathy, and no truth in him. He is a liar, and every word out of his mouth is a lie. He is the father of lies, and there is nothing but falsehood in him. He is a master of deception. His tongue is smoother than fine wine. He is a flatterer. He will make you feel good, while his heart is filled with evil and corruption. Run from that spirit! Flee that spirit! Stay away from that spirit! That spirit is not of God.

The person who says Jesus did come in the flesh is of God. That person has a good spirit, and loves God. Love is in that person, because he or she is born of God. There is a love for God, the house of God, and the people of God. There is no guile in his mouth. There is no deception in his heart. That spirit is of God, and has the character of God. Don't forget to observe the person's action also. Words and action must corroborate.

I think it may be time to go on to what love actually is, now. Let's do that by looking at John 3:16.

What Is Love?

John 3: 16 is the perfect scripture by which to obtain an adequate definition of love. John 3: 16 is love in action. It doesn't merely tell you what love is. It shows you what love is. Let's look at what it has to say.

> "For God so loved the world, He gave his only begotten Son that whosoever believeth in him, would not perish, but will have everlasting life." (John 3:16)

The first phrase in this text is, "For God so loved the world." We derive from the word "so," the extent of love given. You've said that before, too. "I love you so-o-o-o much, indicating how much love you have for someone. Therefore, I think it's safe to surmise that God had a tremendous amount of love for the world.

There's something else we must look at in this scripture, and that's the word "for." Not only did God have a lot of love for the world; that love was a motivator for God to do something. The word "for," can be paraphrased "because." Instead of saying "For God so loved the world…" we can paraphrase that phrase and say, "Because God had so much love for the world…" It definitely shows that love was God's motivation for doing what he did for the world. The first thing we see, then, is that love is a *motivator*. What action does love motivate a person to take? Let's continue, and find out.

Because God loved the world so much, what did love motivate him to do? The text says, "He gave his only begotten son." Love motivated God to *give*. Now, before we go into what God did, let us look at why.

In this text, we don't see God asking for anything. God didn't give to the world because he needed something from the world. God didn't give to the world to grant a request. Neither did God give to the world because he owed the world anything. God doesn't owe us. We owe God! Everything we have, including our lives, has been given to us by God. God didn't give his Son, because he was obligated to the world. He gave his Son because He *wanted* to. Love saw a need, and *took the initiative* to meet it.

Did a light go off? If someone claims to love you, there must be motivation. When love sees a need, no one has to say there's a need. Love steps up to the plate and does what it can to meet that need. No one has to ask. Love takes the *initiative*. It wants to. It has to. That's the nature of love! It can't help it.

The motivation of love caused God to give, which is the *basis* of love. If someone claims to love you, and never gives, you may want to reevaluate that relationship. Giving doesn't have to be money all the time. There are other things to give besides money. You can give your time, your talent, your support, your protection, your affection, or whatever it takes to meet a need.

You may be asking, what did the world need? The need was salvation. We all were on our way to hell, because all of us had sinned, and fallen short of the glory of God. The penalty for sin was death. Still is! We all were facing death, because there was no one to step in and pay the price for our sins. We were destined to pay for our own sins, until God decided to sacrifice his only begotten Son. He saw the need, and took the initiative.

Look at what love motivated God to do. It motivated him to see that we received the *highest good He had for us.* God didn't want us to go to hell. He wanted us to live to worship, serve, and praise him. He wanted us to enjoy the world he created, to live prosperous and happy lives. He wanted us to have the very best.

Ladies, that's what your loved one should want for you—the very best. He may not be able to give you the best. He still should give you the best he can. Love is more than just lip service. Love is *action.* Love is not what you say all the time. Love is what you do.

The next part of this scripture says, "Whosoever believeth in him, should not perish, but will have everlasting life." God didn't give, just to be giving. He gave his Son in order for us to benefit from his giving. Your giving should be *beneficial.* Your giving should be a *blessing.*

Notice that God gave everything he had to meet the need of the world. He didn't give a little, and save something for himself. No! God depleted his resources. He only had one Son, but he freely gave his *only* Son. What he had wasn't as important as the need of the world. The need had to be met, and he was willing to give whatever it took to meet it.

Is your giving helping? Is your giving a blessing? Does it uplift the other person? Look at the benefits in what God gave. The scripture says, "Whosoever believes in him will not perish, but will have everlasting life."

God gave his Son to die for the sins of the world, so the world wouldn't have to pay. Now, look at the real benefits. God says, "If you believe that my Son has died for your sins, you will not perish and go to hell, but will have everlasting life." You won't have to be tormented day and night, for the rest of eternity. Instead, you can go to heaven, and be with the Lord, forever.

Now, let's look at what we've learned from looking at this scripture. First of all, love is a *motivator*. Secondly, love takes the *initiative* to meet the need of the other person. Thirdly, love gives *whatever it takes* to meet the need, even if it costs more than anticipated. Fourthly, what love gives will *benefit the other person tremendously*. What type of definition can we get from this information?

I would say, *"Love is a commitment that is motivated to help the other person receive the very best for his or her life."* Love doesn't think about itself. It thinks about the other person. It actually puts itself on the back burner. It gets its joy from giving, especially when that giving uplifts, meets a need, and puts a smile on the other person's face. Is the person you love putting a smile on your face?

Love is happy when the other person is happy. Just imagine two people doing that for each other. Both will be mutually happy, mutually joyous. It may cost more for one than the other. Nevertheless, the joy of that spiritual connection called love, will ignite, and keep igniting the communion of life in each person. Each day will be as if each person had just met the other, for the first time.

There's no reason why anyone should settle for anything other than the real thing. If it doesn't come from God, you know, now, it isn't love. Treat yourself to the real thing. Experience the everlasting joy of love. Don't settle for momentary pleasure. You, now, know real love comes from God. Don't cheat yourself. God wants the very best for you.

Let us talk about how love looks, now. I know I said love is a spirit. I'm aware you can't see a spirit, with the natural eye. With the spiritual eye, however, you can see the traits of love. The attributes of love are manifested, so you can see them. Remember the old saying? "What's hidden inside a person, will eventually show outside." Love is no different. The character traits of love will be revealed. As someone interacts with you, you'll eventually see what's inside them. Let's see what the true traits of love look like.

CHAPTER 2

WHAT DOES LOVE LOOK LIKE?

I haven't forgotten that I said "love is a spirit." Okay! That's my story, and I'm sticking to it. I'm still going to show you what love looks like. I'm going to show you what an invisible spirit looks like. When I'm finished, you'll know how to recognize love, when you see it. You won't miss out on love again, because you were unable to recognize it. After reading this, you'll know the character of love, and you'll be able to ascertain the attributes of love. Ready? Okay! Here we go.

Every spirit has attributes that are manifested. That is why no one can hide who they really are. Whatever is inside a person, will come out. If love is in a person, the attributes will come out. Then, you'll know if love exists. No one has to believe a person loves them, just because they say so. There are attributes that will be manifested, if love is present. Claims of love will be corroborated, or refuted. The manifestation of the traits of love will be your evidence. Of course, you must know these attributes. That is the only way you will be able to validate love's existence. Let us begin to examine the attributes of love. My point of reference is I Corinthians 13: 1-8.

"Though I speak with the tongues of men and of angels, and have not love, I have become as sounding brass, or a tinkling cymbal. And though I have the gift of prophecy, and understand all mysteries, and all knowledge; and though I have all faith, so that I can move mountains, and have not love, I am nothing. And though I bestow all my goods to feed the poor, and though I give my body to be burned, and have not charity, it profiteth me nothing."

I'll get into the attributes of love in a minute. I just want to say a little bit about the first three (3) verses of the above mentioned scripture. I think it's necessary to say something about this, because people will try to impress you with their talents and skills, to make you fall in love with them. It happens all the time. Don't be deceived.

If you fall in love with someone because he sings good, and he knocks you off your feet, that's not love, that's *infatuation*. Look at what God is telling you. He is saying that just because a person can speak in the tongues of men and angels, without love in his heart, he's just making noise, like sounding brass and a tinkling cymbal. Where is the desire to help people with those skills and talents? Are they glorifying God? Talent and skill can fascinate you. Still, that's not love. You can become infatuated with a person, without ever knowing who that person is.

Intelligence may fascinate you also. Ladies, don't run away and elope, because his mind is so brilliant. You will be sorry you did. Nobody wants an ignorant mate, but to love someone based on intelligence alone, will end in disappointment. The fascination in one's intelligence may make you swoon, but have you ever stopped to consider what's being done with it? Who is it helping besides the person who possesses it? Without love, the accumulation of knowledge fails to make a person significant. People are blessed with gifts to be a blessing to others. If not, what's the use?

The last thing I have to talk about is the generous person, the one who gives to charity. They feed the poor, and make personal sacrifices to people less fortunate than themselves. They seem generous, on the surface. Are they? Many people give generously, because they need tax deductions. Is it really the poor they are concerned about, or is it their bottom line. What am I saying?

I'm saying, there is nothing wrong with loving the talented, the intelligent, or the generous. However, the Bible says, that even when one is endowed with such great qualities, they profit nothing, without love. They're not useful, serviceable, or advantageous, because without love, those gifts are useless, and profit nothing. Besides, the gift is not the person. Get to know the person. See what God has placed within him. If love is there, it'll come out. Others will see it. You'll see it. Love cannot be hidden.

Okay! I have beat around the bush long enough. Let's dive into the rest of 1 Corinthians 13; 1-8, and see how love really looks. I have already talked about verses 1-3. Now, I shall discuss verses 4-8. This is going to be so good! You'll recognize love, after this. You're going to be so confident. I promise! Okay. Here we go. The traits of love are as follows:

Patience:

1 Corinthians 13: 4 says, "Love suffereth long." Actually, the Greek word used for love is charity. I shall use the word love in my explanations, as to not get lost in translation. When you look at the phrase suffereth long, it would appear that love must exist in hurt and pain. Not so! Many people do believe that, unfortunately.

The word suffereth here is not the type of suffering we are familiar with. The actual Greek translation for suffereth is "patience." This verse is saying that love is long-spirited, and forebearing. In other words, love hangs in there whenever trouble, disappointment, or misfortune arises.

Love endures atrocities. Love does not leave the other person, and throw in the towel. Love stays right there, in the thick of it. Love takes the ridicule, the smirks, and the offenses. The lies told on love may hurt, but love still endures. The Bible says to "Wait on the Lord." That's what love does. It waits patiently on the Lord. Ever been abandoned by the one who said he loved you? That was not love. Love waits to see what the end will be.

The patience of love also includes temperance. Love doesn't lose its temper, easily. Why? Love has faith in God. Love does not depend on itself. Love depends on God. I am not saying love does not get angry. It does! Patience, however, keeps love from sinning. When hope is in that in which you cannot see, you patiently wait on it. Love has its hope and trust in God. Love does not correct, or resolve. Love lets God do that.

Kindness:

There seems to be a prevalent idea that love hurts. Where that came from, I have no idea. I have never believed that, but I have been in relationships with women who did. They believed that if love didn't hurt, it wasn't real. Because of that belief, they didn't like being treated nicely. They preferred to be disrespected, insulted, abused, and humiliated. Some women are like that, today. Go figure!

Contrary to popular belief, the Bible says love is *kind*. Love doesn't hurt. The Greek word for kindness is "chrestotes," which means uprightness, goodness, and generosity. In other words, love treats the other person nicely, is generous in giving, and is righteous in its conduct. Love is not abusive!

Kindness is considered a weakness, today, especially if it comes from a man. I've seen good men dumped by women who said kindness was boring. They liked the *"bad boy."* I was told, by various women, the bad boy is unpredictable, and that makes him more exciting. On the other hand, the nice guy is too predictable, which makes him boring.

The bad boy curses his woman, when he feels she hasn't done what she should've done. The nice guy forgives his woman, when she makes a mistake. The bad guy is selfish, and always thinks about himself. The nice guy puts the needs of his lady first. The bad guy cheats on his woman. The nice guy doesn't cheat. The bad guy continuously belittles his woman in public. The nice guy encourages his woman, and lifts her self-esteem. He makes her feel important. Which one of these would you choose? Kindness looks best to me.

No one can receive the kindness of love unless they have the spirit of love in him. People prefer abuse rather than love, because they don't appreciate themselves. Their self-esteem is low. Abuse won't be tolerated, when a woman loves herself. I don't know about you, but I would rather have kindness. I mean, if I have to be abused, to have excitement, you can have it! If I have to be humiliated, to be appreciated, you can have it. Give me kindness any day.

No Envy:

The next trait of love is "no envy." The Bible says, "love envieth not" (1 Corinthians. 13: 4). The Greek word for envy is "zeloo," which means to be *zealously against, or to covet*. The word zealous indicates enthusiasm. There is a certain level of energy exerted, when a person is envious. There is an eagerness to have what you have. It's a zestful feeling of ill will, an eagerness to hurt. That's not love!

A person who is zealously against another hates to see that person blessed. Have you ever seen someone hate another person for no reason? Usually, the person hated has achieved something the hater wanted to achieve. Often, the hated person has something the hater wants, but is unable to get. When the hated person receives accolades from others, a hater feels those compliments should have been his. Subsequently, the hatred of the hater intensifies, because not only does he hate the hated, he also hates those who loves the person he hates.

Love doesn't covet what the other person has. Covetousness is *greed*. When a person is envious, they are not satisfied with what God has blessed them. They want what others have, as well. They want to appear superior, in the eyes of others. They want to be accepted. Deeply inside, however, there is a feeling of *inferiority*. Therefore, they put others down to make themselves look good, even those they say they love.

Envy can be lethal. It can cause a person to commit murder. Remember Cain and his brother Abel, in Genesis 4: 1-9? Both, he and his brother, offered sacrifices to God. His brother's offering was accepted by God, but his wasn't. Cain killed his brother, because he was envious of his brother. Cain felt rejected and inferior, and committed the first murder, in the history of the world.

So, watch the envious types. If they have a tendency to put you down, to make themselves look good. Run! If they hate you because you have acquired things they wanted, but could never get. Run! Love is happy when the other person is blessed. Love will help you celebrate your blessing. Love envies not.

Conceit and Pride:

The Bible says, "Love vaunteh not itself, is not puffed up." The Greek meaning for "vaunt" is to be *conceited or boastful*. A conceited person is a person who thinks more highly of himself than he should. He brags and boasts about himself. Everything is about him. The Bible talks about a person like that in Galatians. 6:3: "For if a man think himself to be something, when he is nothing, he deceiveth himself." In other words, that person is living in a fantasy world. Nothing in that world is real. He may want it to be real. Unfortunately, it isn't.

If a person lives in a fantasy world, how can the love he declares be real? It isn't real, because it's only in his mind. It's imagination. He desires it, but deceives himself that he has it. His love is only something he brags about. Unfortunately, it isn't real. The only function of that fantasy is to make him look good, or feel good. What a life of pretense and fraudulence! Who wants someone, that lives a phony life? It would be amazing if he even knows who he is.

The other part of this character trait is pride. Remember, the verse says, "love vaunteth not itself, and is not puffed up?" Let's talk about the "puffed up" part that deals with pride. The Greek meaning for puffed up is "pride." No one wants a person filled with pride. Trust me! If God hates pride (Proverbs 6:17), you shouldn't fall in love with a person like that. Let me tell you why you shouldn't.

A person filled with pride is an idolater. He worships himself. No one else is right but him. No one is better than he is, more beautiful than he is, or smarter than he is. Where God should be, the person filled with pride has elevated himself to that spot. Not only does this person worship himself, he expects everyone else to do the same. That also includes his significant other. If that doesn't happen, he feels his significant other doesn't love him, and isn't loyal to him. A person with pride will discard you like a bad habit, and won't look back. Get away!

Okay! I think that is enough about that particular trait. Let's move on to the next one. We still have a ways to go.

No Indecency, No Shame

The next character trait is in verse five (5) of 1 Corinthians 13. It says that love "doth not behave itself unseemly." The Greek meaning for unseemly is *"indecency that leads to shame."* Love doesn't dishonor the other person. It will not embarrass, humiliate, or bring shame upon the other person. To the contrary, love is respectful, and makes the other person feel valuable. It doesn't insult, belittle, or embarrass. Love doesn't make a spectacle of itself, or the other person.

If a person says they love you, and they constantly bring shame upon you, that isn't love. Love values the other person too much to insult the relationship. Love doesn't conduct itself in an indecent way. Love will not cheat on you with your sister, get her pregnant, and ask her to have an abortion, to cover it up. You will not see love on the six o'clock news in handcuffs, because he got arrested for attempting to rob the local bank. You won't come home and find love in the bed you sleep in, with another person. Love will not bring shame or dishonor upon the other person. Love will always behave in a moral, honorable, and decent way.

If you are, however, in that type of relationship, don't hold your head down, and think yourself less than who you are. Just get out of it, and remember: God created you, and you are "fearfully and wonderfully made" (Psalms 139: 14). Give God praise for how he has made you. You are uniquely, respectfully, and beautifully made. Since you are made by Almighty God, you are a designer's original. There is no one else like you.

When God created you, he broke the mold. That means you are special. There's nothing average about you, because there are no copies of you. You stand alone! You are unique! There are no flaws in your design. An expert did the creativity. You're just like God intended you to be. Rejoice! Don't accept humiliation, or embarrassment. You are a child of God. You are special!

Not Selfish:

The next trait of love this scripture talks about is selfishness. The text says that love "seeketh not her own." Love doesn't look out for itself. Love is committed to the other person. When a person only thinks about himself, that person is selfish. A good way to detect a selfish person is how he uses his personal pronouns. If he always says I, me, mine, and my, instead of ours, us, or we, most likely that person is selfish. His concern isn't the relationship. His concern is himself, and how the relationship can benefit him.

If you aren't cautious, a selfish person can make you an *idolater*. Ladies, what I mean is, that person will make you worship him, making you think you must please him, and only him. Before you know it, your life will consist of nothing more than doing what he says, going where he says, wearing what he says, and saying what he tells you to say. You won't have a will of your own any longer, because he will have put you in *bondage*. He will have exclusive control over your mind. That's not love! Be cautious ladies.

Always remember this! The foundation of love is *giving*. It sacrifices for the other person. Love doesn't get what it needs, and leaves the other person in want. Love meets the need of the other person first. No one has to tell love his significant other is in need. Love stays abreast of what the other person needs, and does all he can to meet that need. Love is not stingy!

Ladies, if you are in a relationship, and you are always giving, but are never receiving anything, that's a one-sided relationship. The only person benefiting from that relationship is the one on the receiving end. It may be a good thing to sit down and have a face-to-face with your significant other, and tell him how his lack of giving makes you feel.

Love is sacrificial. Love can't help but give. Giving is a part of love's nature. It gives without keeping track of what it gives. Love will give its all to make the other person happy. Giving shows you care. When a person cares, he shows it by giving. Isn't that what God did? He gave his *only* Son. He made a huge sacrifice for who he loved, and it cost him everything. If he hadn't made that sacrifice, we wouldn't have eternal life. We would still be in our sins, on our way to hell. Hallelujah! I'm glad love sacrifices, and seeks not her own.

Okay! Let us continue with the other traits of love.

Not Easily Provoked:

This phrase simply means *love is not touchy, irritable, or easily angered*. Have you ever been around someone who loses his temper every time you say something? What you say doesn't have to be anything drastic or threatening. The lack of self-control causes him to get angry, because he operates on a short fuse. When a person is unable to control his emotions, he can be an irritable person with whom no one wants to associate. Your friends will decline to hang out with you, if they know Mr. Lack-of-Control is going to be present.

An irritable person likes to argue. Everything can be perfectly quiet, and that person will find something to argue about. Ever been around someone like that? If you go on a date with a person like that, be careful. There could be loud outbursts about nothing at all, and you could be totally embarrassed and humiliated. Mr. Lack-of-Control may cause onlookers to stare at you, whisper about you, and move away from you, for a more peaceful surrounding. That's not a good portrait of love, and it can happen to both men and women.

Love is not so touchy, you can't communicate. Communication, when love is present, is very intimate. Conversation touches the heart and the spirit of a person. It helps two people to know each other better, and causes them to get closer. It's part of the process of becoming one flesh. I know what you are thinking. You're thinking it takes sex for two people to become one flesh. That isn't so! You can become one flesh in your goals, your aspirations, your ideas, your beliefs, your emotions, your likes, and in even your dislikes.

The flesh is merely referring to the nature of man, not the skin of man. Our nature is who we are, as human beings. Communication connects two people, because words, along with the emotions that accompany them, draw people together. When one human nature relates to another, words are the medium that *joins* people together. Speak those words that edify, and you'll become like each other. You'll have each other's strength.

On the other hand, constant angry outbursts *repel*. The loudness of bitterness doesn't draw others to you. To the contrary, it makes others avoid you, run from you, and shun you. An irritable person has a difficult time sharing love, because he is so easily provoked. When love is shared, there's a comfort that makes the other person want to be in your presence. Irritability does the opposite. It makes a person not want to be in your presence. Pray for self-control.

Thinks No Evil:

This phrase has a different meaning other than what seemingly appears. The word *thinks* may look as if a person has evil on his mind constantly, always thinking about what is evil. The western connotation of this phrase would have you think a person continuously contemplates bad things to do. For instance, thinking of killing someone, robbing a bank, or committing adultery with your best friend's wife. You would scheme, plot, and plan for those things. They would always be on your mind. Get my drift? Well, that isn't what this phrase is referring to.

When the Bible says, love "thinketh no evil," it's actually talking about keeping a ledger of the wrong done to it, in order to hold it over someone's head. Love doesn't *judge, in order to condemn.* Love forgives. It doesn't hold grudges, waiting for the right time to bring something up that may be 5 or 6 years old. You can easily develop a guilt complex in a relationship like that, always hearing about your mistakes, your failures, or what you did wrong. When that happens, you'll begin to think you have to act a certain way, in order to be accepted. Your life will be miserable, because you'll live seeking someone else's approval, which you'll never get. You'll never be able to please that person. They'll always be ready to remind you, from the ledger they keep, of what you did in the past. It would be a life of walking on egg shells.

If a person is unable to forgive, and let things go, get away from them. An unforgiving person will forever harbor anger and bitterness. They'll hold on to grudges. Eventually, that person will do something to satisfy his grudge, by devising a way to get even. An unforgiving person usually wants the person that hurt them to hurt, too. They hold on to the past, in order to accuse you, hoping to condemn you. That's not love. Love *thinketh* no evil.

Rejoices Not In Iniquity,
But Rejoices In The Truth:

We live in a world wherein the *players syndrome* is prevalent. If you've heard of a player, but don't know what it is, let's talk about that lifestyle for a minute. Many women like men, who are players.

A player is a person who lives by a fabricated body of knowledge called *game*. The game is a code filled with *deceit, trickery, and lies*. This body of lies is never the same. It depends on who the player is, and what his objective is. Suffice it to say, game is how the player gets what he wants.

When it comes to love, players don't fall in love. Usually, they aren't born of God. Therefore, the spirit of God, which is also the spirit of love, isn't in them. Consequently, they live by iniquity, which is a way of lawlessness. They live by their own rules.

Players don't fall in love, because they don't make commitments. They lie to one woman, in order to see another. They cheat! Players are never tied down to just one person. They live a lifestyle of selfishness, and are skillful in making iniquities [unlawful things] come to pass. As a result of their selfish deception, the other person usually gets hurt. That, of course, doesn't bother the player. His concern is being true to the game. He can't afford to let his feelings get involved. To him, that shows weakness. You only see a player when he has time for you. He won't let you get emotionally close.

The appalling thing today is women seem to like the player type. Every woman doesn't call him player, though. Some refer to him as *bad boy*. I asked a few women why they preferred the player over the good guy. They replied by saying that the player is unpredictable, and that makes him exciting, and fun. On the other hand, the good guy is too predictable. That much familiarity makes him boring. What is wrong with expecting kindness and good treatment?

Let me understand this. Because the player, or the bad boy, is exciting, women are willing to put up with his lies and deception? Knowing the bad boy cheated on you, and continues to do so, is tolerated just to keep excitement in your life? That's crazy! Being treated right doesn't seem important anymore. Does excitement supersede respect? How can a woman think a man, who treats her that way, loves her?

Love doesn't use iniquity to control the other person. Love is honest. How can being truthful be boring? I don't know about you, but I would be happy knowing I was with someone who didn't intend to deceive me, or use me, or hurt me. That would be exciting! Unfortunately, that's not the world we live in. Why someone would like being deceived is beyond me. Isn't that a little masochistic? Look at what's in store for the player.

> "Woe unto the world because of offences! For it must needs that offences come; but woe to the man by whom the offences come." (Matthew 18: 7)

Let's unpack the above scripture, as we move further into this discussion.

The word *offence* means *"to cause to stumble."* The player, because he operates by iniquity, causes those affiliated with him to stumble. Stumbling entails living contrary to how God wants you to live. It also includes being who God did not intend you to be. Love doesn't seek to make a person stumble from the destiny God has for them, and rejoices about it. Love doesn't rejoice in that type of transgression.

God wants you to walk in righteousness. Offences make you stumble. When stumbling takes place, people become personalities they were never meant to be, and they do things contrary to what God wants them to do.

Do you think God meant for a woman to be a stripper, prostitute, or drug addict? No! They were caused to stumble from what God wanted them to be. They are created to worship and serve God, not to please men who make wicked devices come to pass. Evil men boast about how they made women to stumble, and at what they created them to be. "Man, that's mine. I turned her out. Got her from the projects. Ain't she bad? She makes more money than anyone on the strip. I put my brand on her." That's not love. That's abuse!

Rejoice in the truth, not iniquity. Praise God for how he made you, and do all you can to be what he wants you be. Then, you'll live a righteous life, a life that glorifies God.

The last portion of the above scripture says that there is a penalty for causing offences, or making others stumble. It says that offences will come, but "woe unto the man by whom the offences come." There is a *woe* attached to the person by whom the offence comes. The word woe means *"an exclamation of grief."* Those who make others stumble, will experience grief.

> "But whoso shall offend one of these little ones
> which believe in me, it were better for him that
> a millstone were hanged about his neck and
> that he were drowned in the depth of the sea."
> (Matthew. 18:6)

The above scripture says that causing another person to stumble, and lose their faith in God, is looked upon badly by God. Regarding the individual who does that, the Bible says that it would be better that a millstone were hanged about his neck, and he be drowned in the bottom of the sea. Those who say they love someone, but makes them stumble, this text says it would be better they were dead, than having done that. For the judgment they'll face will be exceedingly worse. Love doesn't rejoice in iniquity. It rejoices in truth. If not, there's a price to pay. Love doesn't bring you down. It picks you up.

Beareth All Things:

The Greek meaning of this phrase is, *"to protect, or preserve by covering."* Love is a shelter that covers the other person, in order to keep them safe. Anything that threatens the other person, love protects them from it. Regardless of what is said or done, love is not swayed. Love takes the gossip, the rumors, the accusations, the reproaches, and the slander, covering the other person from the hurt, the humiliation, and the shame.

Men, love is loyal. It doesn't run, and leave the other person alone, to bear her burdens by herself. Love helps her bear her burdens. Even for those things that come to destroy the other person, love has a covering that protects.

The best example of *"bearing all things"* would be Jesus. He loved us so, he protected us from the destination of hell by covering us from the penalty of sin. Instead, he bore the pain of that penalty, which is death, on the cross. What is the result of that covering? Our status is now changed from sinner to saint. Our destination has also been changed from hell to heaven.

Anyone declaring love for another must bear all things. The other person must know there is someone there who won't leave them to bear their burdens alone. Protection must be there to preserve them. Love doesn't sit by and watch troublesome things destroy the other person. It *beareth* all things.

Believeth All Things:

The Greek meaning of this phrase is *"to commit to one's trust."* This doesn't mean that love believes everything the other person says. It means that the other person is persuaded that they can trust you. A person must be committed to trusting the person they love. If a person says they love you, you should be able to trust them. You should be *convinced* you can trust them. No one can tell you the person who loves you, doesn't love you, because you are persuaded they do. You trust, and are committed to, the love they declare for you.

There's nothing more frustrating than to be in love with someone, and not be sure of their love. That type of uncertainty prevents you from being happy. It isn't reliable. You can' be committed to it. That isn't something you have to worry about, regarding love, though. You can trust it, rely upon it, and be committed to it. Skepticism and love don't interact.

Hopeth All Things:

The Greek meaning of this phrase means *"to anticipate the best."* When a person is in a relationship, he expects certain things from love. This anticipation isn't a critical expectation that reprimands someone who doesn't do, or be, what you expected. To the contrary, this type of hope is in the growth of the other person. You look for them to be all that God wants them to be. There's an anticipation of good in every facet of the other person's life.

Love believes in you. It has faith in you. Without faith, there can be no hope. Love hopes the best for the other person. Not only does love hope the best, it anticipates the best. If you've been told, by someone, they love you, but doesn't hope the best for you, that's not love. Love hopes the best health, prosperity, home, family relations, spiritual life, and social relations.

Stay away from negative people. They tend to have no hope. Pessimism is a way of life for them. Love isn't like that. Love believes in the good. It looks for the good. It looks for the best. It expects the best. Love *hopeth* all things.

Endureth All Things:

This phrase has to do with *fortitude and resilience.* We've vaguely touched on this already, but love *perseveres.* Love is strong. It doesn't waver in strength. It's always strong, and stays there for the other person. Love gives support. You can lean on love, and trust that leaning post to be sturdy. Love isn't weak.

When troublesome difficulties arise in your life, you should be able to depend on love. Love isn't in a hurry for problems to be resolved. Love is patient when the other person is suffering. You never hear love say, "This is taking too long. Call me when there's a change." No! Love endureth all things.

Never Fails:

The Greek meaning of this phrase is *"to drop away, or to fall out of."* If God never fails, it's logical that love never fails either, since God is love. Love doesn't drop away, and you don't fall out of love.

You're always hearing people say that love let them down. Subsequently, they stop believing in it. That's unfortunate, because love never fails. Either they misunderstood love, or they never had a grasp on what love really does.

You may have heard some women say, "I don't love my husband anymore. I've fallen out of love with him." That isn't possible! You can't fall out of a spirit. You can only *reject* it. When two people are joined together, that's forever. The only way that relationship can be broken is by rejection. How can you fall out of something that lives inside of you? The spirit didn't leave you. You left the spirit. You rejected it!

Love doesn't take a break. It doesn't *"drop away."* Love never stops loving. You hear people say, "I need some space." Well, space doesn't stop the existence of love. Often, people try to run from love. That's like running from God. Where can you go to escape the presence of God? He's omnipresent! God is everywhere, at the same time. Come on!

Love, like God, is not coercive. It doesn't force itself on anyone. You must exercise your will. Love doesn't make anyone accept it. Love merely makes itself accessible and available. People fail to realize that when you accept love, you accept God. When two people are joined together by love, they're also joined together by God. When you reject love, you also reject God.

When a woman leaves a man who truly loves her, everybody laughs at him. They say he was not strong enough to hold his woman. That may be a general consensus, but that's not true. I used to believe that, too. I found out for myself. That's not true.

A man is not less a man, when a woman leaves him. He's only different. The woman simply rejects the spirit in the man. If she's looking for love, and he doesn't possess it, her leaving is logical. If he does possess love, and she's looking for a bad boy, her leaving is equally logical.

That woman is just looking for a compatible spirit. That doesn't make the man she left, less of a man. He's only different. One thing is certain, however. If the woman did reject love, she also rejected God. Her leaving doesn't mean love failed her. She just didn't want it. Not wanting love does not negate its power. Love does not drop away. People drop away. Love never fails.

"And now abides faith, hope, love, these three; but
the greatest of these is love." (1Corinthians. 13:13)

Now that you know how love looks, you should not be
heartbroken again, or betrayed. You should be able to identify love
when you see it. You now have the ability to, not only ascertain,
but validate love.

Stay tuned. We're, now, going to discuss the different types
of love.

CHAPTER 3

STORGE

The Greek word "storge" means *family love*. The only requirement for this type of love is to be a part of the family. This type of love is blood related. If you have the family bloodline, you are in the family, and are eligible to receive family love. It is not necessary to have God's spirit to be in this type of family. This type of family is purely biological. Every member of the family is joined together by the family's bloodline.

Because the family bloodline is the only necessity, love relations can fluctuate. They fluctuate because they are activated by *human will*. Feelings go in and out. They are never the same. Toleration goes in and out also. You never relate the same way, to the same people, each day. There is no regulation, because the spirit of love is not present.

It's idealistic for an entire family to be saved, though not impossible. However, most families consist of both, the saved and the unsaved. When the family structure is like that, there's conflict between the two different spirits. Look at what God's word says about that. Maybe, then, you can understand why there's so much conflict in the families you see around you.

"But if you bite and devour one another, take heed that ye be not consumed one of another. This I say then, Walk in the spirit, and ye shall not fulfill the lust of the flesh. For the flesh lusteth against the Spirit, and the Spirit against the flesh; and these are contrary the one to the other; so that ye cannot do the things that ye would." (Galatians 5: 15-17)

As you can see from the above scripture, the saved and the unsaved have different spirits that oppose each other. That's how it is when the structure of the family is made of different spirits. That's why it's so important to share the gospel of Jesus Christ with your family. When everyone has the spirit of God, not only will love be present in the family, peace and harmony will also be present.

When a person is saved, he receives God's spirit. That spirit, as we have already discovered, is love. Family members who have not received the spirit of God, have the spirit of the world. The world *hates* the spirit of God. Those in that spirit are friends of the world, which makes them enemies of God (James 4:4). They hate the things of God, and are not drawn to them. They oppose them, because they are foolishness to them. So, what they love is contrary to the things those, who are saved, love. They are still in the biological family, but they are not in the family of God. That creates conflict. When unsaved family members do things to hurt their saved relatives, it's not the person they hate, it's the God, in that person, they hate.

When a person is saved, he is still in the world, but he isn't of the world. He doesn't live by the principles of the world. The Word of God is what leads him, along with the Holy Spirit. Herein is the conflict between saved and unsaved family members. The principles each one lives by is different, not to mention in opposition to one another. Here are some examples.

1. The unsaved member may think it okay to fornicate. The saved one does not.
2. The unsaved member sees nothing wrong in driving with a suspended driving license. The saved one does.
3. The unsaved sees nothing wrong in gambling at the casino, and possibly losing the house mortgage. The saved one does.
4. The unsaved member sees nothing wrong with cheating on his taxes, if you can get away with it. The saved one does.
5. The saved member will lie on another person, and get them in trouble, to save himself. The saved one will not.

When a friend of mine was called to preach the gospel, his family didn't believe it. They didn't believe it because, before he was called to preach, he lived by the principles of the world. He did the same things his family did. He went to the clubs, chased women, smoked marijuana, was in and out of jail, and ran the streets all night. That's the person they knew, and for him to be a preacher seemed ludicrous. Even his mother was reluctant to believe it.

He began to travel a different path than his family. He went to church more. His family thought he was going through a phase. He would snap out of it soon, they thought. Well, after six years passed, and my friend finished seminary, and was called to pastor his first church, their eyes were opened. Still, they went separate ways. The family still didn't want anything to do with that *God stuff.* Their lives were still governed by the principles of the world. Look at the following scripture. God can say so much more than I can.

"A man's foes shall be they of his own household."
(Matthew 10:36)

Remember the story of Cain and Abel? They were brothers, with the same mother and father. They had the same bloodline. Cain lived in the flesh, but Abel was more spiritual. Both made an offering to God. Abel's offering was accepted, but Cain's offering was rejected. Jealously entered into Cain, and he killed his brother, Abel.

It looked like Cain would have been happy for his brother. After all, they were family. They grew up in the same home. They were raised by the same parents. They shared the same bloodline. All the time they were growing up, Cain lusted against Abel. The Bible doesn't say if Abel knew how Cain felt about him. Nevertheless, the hatred was there.

We would all like our family members to love us. I am not trying to be negative, but blood relations alone cannot ensure peace and love. The spirit of love must be present, in order for love to exist. Let's look at another family that fits the above scripture. Joseph was also hated by his family.

Jacob, Joseph's father, had twelve sons. Joseph was his favorite, because Joseph was the son of his old age. To show his love for Joseph, Jacob made a coat of many colors for him. The other sons were jealous. They became furiously jealous when Joseph told them his dream. The dream revealed all of them in the fields gathering sheaves. The sheaves of the eleven brothers bowed down to Joseph's sheaves, as if they were worshipping Joseph.

When Joseph told the dream to his brothers, they were livid. They were already angry because of the coat. Now, Joseph was telling them that, one day, they would bow down and worship him. Of course, the dream was prophetic, and came from God. Still, the other brothers were extremely angry, to think Joseph thought them to be subordinate to him.

The brothers wanted to kill Joseph, but one of them talked the group out of it. So, they decided to throw Joseph in a pit. They sold him to a caravan passing by. To cover up what they had done, they put the blood of and animal on Joseph's coat of many colors. When they got home, they told their father a wild animal had devoured him.

It appears that, in both stories, jealousy is the source of hatred. That's not odd, though. That's scriptural. Remember the scripture in Galatians 5? It said, "the flesh lusted against the spirit, and the spirit against the flesh, and they were contrary one to the other." Even though the family blood flowed through every member of the family, the spirits did not agree with each other. Both harbored desires against each other. One was for evil, and one for good.

Fellowship comes from the compatibility of spirits. Remember that, when seeking a love relationship. You have things in common when you have the same spirit. Haven't you noticed how people of like spirits hang with each other? People are joined together by the spirits that live within them. All lying spirits hang together. All spirits of greed hang together. Christians hang together. All lustful spirits hang together. We, as humans, are spirits, not just bodies. Who we are is inside our bodies.

It is apparent that mere bloodlines can't produce unity in the family. When there are different spirits under one roof, there are actually two families living there. *There is an earthly family, and there is a heavenly family.* The unsaved family members make up the earthly family. The saved family members make up the heavenly family.

The earthly family lives in the flesh. It has no connection to the things of God, and cares not for the things of God. The flesh is selfish, and only cares about pleasing itself. It doesn't care for the others. The flesh, which is nothing but our human nature, cannot do what is morally right. It doesn't have the ability to live in a righteous manner. It may want to love but to actually do it; it doesn't have the power to do so. Let's look at the Word of God, and see what is said about that.

"For that which I do I allow not: for what I would, that do I not; but what I hate, that I do. If then I do that which I would not, I consent unto the law that it is good. Now then it is no more I that do it, but sin that dwelleth in me. For I know that in me (that is, in my flesh,) dwelleth no good thing: for to will is present with me; but how to perform that which is good I find not. For the good that I would I do not: but the evil which I would not, that I do. Now if I do that I would not, it is no more I that do it, but sin that dwelleth in me. I find then a law, that, when I would do good, evil is present with me." (Romans 7: 15-21)

As you can see from the above text, they who are influenced by the flesh may want to do what is right, but how to perform it continuously escapes them. What they want to do, they end up not doing, but end up doing what they hate. It's not them who do it. It's the sin that lives in their flesh.

The above scripture says there is nothing good in human nature (the flesh). There's a will that wants to do what is right, but how to perform what is right is never discovered. The unsaved family members may want to do the right thing, but they fail to discover how to perform what is right. There is no guidance from the Holy Spirit. Therefore, how to love is not present. They may want to, but they just can't do it.

There are certain character traits the flesh conveys. When the bible says, "It is not me, but sin that lives in me," the following traits are what that refers to. This is what embodies human nature. These are the fruit and character of the flesh.

Adultery   Wrath
Fornication   Strife

Uncleanness	Seditions
Lasciviousness	Heresies
Idolatry	Envyings
Witchcraft	Murders
Hatred	Drunkenness
Variance	Revellings
Emulations	...and the like

(Galatians 5: 19-21). If you noticed, love isn't on that list. Sex is, but not love.

The traits of the family member, who has God's spirit, are different.

They are as follows:

Love	Joy	Peace
Longsuffering (patience)	Gentleness	Goodness
Faith	Meekness	Temperance (self-control)

If you noticed, love is at the top of that list. It's easy to see that those lists are very different. Both represent the character of two different people. Which person would you say is easier to get along with? Which person would you trust? Which person would you say has love in them? If you chose the bottom list, which represents the person with God's spirit, you are correct. Look at what the Word of God says about the people of both lists.

> "For they that are after the flesh do mind the things of the flesh; but they that are after the Spirit the things of the Spirit. For to be carnally minded is death; but to be spiritually minded is

life and peace. Because the carnal mind is enmity against God; for it is not subject to the law of God, neither indeed can be. So then they that are in the flesh cannot please God." (Romans 8: 5-8)

The carnal minded person lives in accordance to his own human nature. He is guided by it. The Bible calls him a dead man. Those who live in the spirit, however, have life and peace. They who are carnally minded are hostile, and are in opposition to God. They're not subject to the word of God. It's impossible for them to be so. There's no way they can please God. The only way to change a person like that is to share with them the gospel of Jesus Christ. That's the power of God that renders salvation. Until they receive salvation, they'll never have the capacity to love.

Many carnal minded people may argue, 'I do love my family." Well, you may think you do. Unless you are filled with the Holy Ghost, the spirit of love is not present in you. What you are sharing is only human affection, because true love comes from God. Without him living inside you, love is not present. No one can love by his own strength.

I realize I am talking about blood relatives. Blood relations just aren't enough to produce unity and love in the family. That's why the goal of every family member should be to see his family give their lives to Christ, and be filled with the Holy Spirit. Then, you can say you have a family filled with love.

It isn't enough to merely be in the biological family. All of us should want our families to be saved. Sure! We want our families to love each other. More than that, though, is the destination of our families. Will this time on earth be the last time you see your family? We should want or families to go to heaven. There, we will see them again.

When we die, all of us will spend eternity somewhere, heaven or hell. Heaven is where God is. I don't know about you, but I want to be where God is. You can't get there through osmosis, though. You must accept Jesus Christ as Lord and Savior. Look at what the Word of God says about this.

> "For whosoever shall call upon the name of the Lord shall be saved. How then shall they call on him in whom they have not believed? and how shall they believe in him of whom they have not heard? and how shall they hear without a preacher? (Romans 10: 13-14

This scripture says that anybody can be saved, if they call upon the name of the Lord. This means that anyone in your family can be saved. All they have to do is call upon the name of the Lord. Of course, they must get to the point they want salvation. It's just like a drug addict. Unless he wants to be healed, he won't be healed. It's the same way with salvation. If a person wants to be saved, they can be saved. All they have to do is call upon the name of the Lord, and tell him they want to be saved.

Before your family member can call upon the name of the Lord, they must believe in him. The above scripture says that before they can believe, they must hear the gospel of Jesus Christ. "Faith (believing) comes by hearing, and hearing by the word of God" (Romans 10: 17). Until they hear about Jesus, they won't have a reason to believe on him. Faith is produced by believing the Word of God. Your family must, first, believe that Jesus died on the cross for their sins, that he was raised from the dead, and that he is coming back again. Then, they can call on the name of the Lord.

You ask, maybe, how will your family hear the gospel? The first thing that usually comes to mind is, from the preacher. When we think of the word preacher, we think of the office of a preacher. We fail to think of the activity of a preacher.

Ordinary people in the family don't have the office of preacher. They can, however, execute the activity of a preacher, which is to proclaim. You don't have to proclaim the gospel from a pulpit, in order for your family to believe the word, and be saved.

I know the scripture asks, "How shall they hear without a preacher?" Every witness is not in a pulpit. You can be a witness to your family. You can proclaim the gospel of Jesus to your family.

Your first witnessing tool is your life. If you believe in the gospel you intend to share with your family, your life should be a sermon. People are more prone to believe a sermon they can see, rather than a sermon they can hear. Often, people say one thing and do another. They are known as *hypocrites*. Make sure your life exemplifies the gospel, before you share it with someone. You don't have to be perfect, to be a witness for the Lord. You just have to be faithful. With patience and prayer, you can help your family be saved.

Someone mentioned to me that he didn't feel connected to his family. Because he was saved, and his family was not, he felt distant. He loved his family, but he didn't feel his family loved him. They all had the same bloodline, but there was no family unity or cohesiveness. Look at the following scripture. It speaks about that also.

> "There came then his brethren and his mother, and, standing without, sent unto him, calling him. And the multitude sat about him, Behold, thy mother and thou brethren without seek for thee. And he answered them, saying, Who is my mother, or my brethren? And he looked round about them which sat about him, and said, Behold my mother and my brethren! For whosoever shall do the will of God, the same is my brother, and my sister, and my mother." (Mark 3: 31-35)

In the above-mentioned scripture, Jesus is confirming what I have previously said. Blood lineage does not make a family. Let's go a little deeper.

While Jesus was teaching the multitude, his mother and brothers came to the place where he was, and asked for him. Jesus was told his mother and brothers were outside, and wanted to see him. Now, look at Jesus' reply. "Who is my mother and my brothers?" he asked. Then, he looked around at the people who were there to hear his teaching, and said, "Look! These are my mother and my brothers. Whoever does the will of God, those are my mother and my brothers."

Let me tell you a little story, and maybe you will understand why Jesus didn't consider his earthly family his real family.

When God created Adam and Eve, he endowed them with eternal life. He created them in his image and after his likeness. They were a part of God's family. At that time, death and sin hadn't entered into the world. Everything belonged to them, but God gave them one commandment. He told them not to eat from the tree in the middle of the garden, or they would surely die.

Satan, an enemy of God, deceived Eve, and persuaded her to disobey God's commandment. She ate from the tree God told her not to eat from. She influenced her husband to eat, and he ate also. At that time, death and sin entered into the world, and Adam and Eve lost eternal life, and were no longer in the family of God. Because of them, we were born with a sin nature, and death, which is the penalty of sin, came upon us all. Something had to be done.

As a result of Adam and Eve's disobedience, we are born with a sin nature, with death hanging over our heads. That's why God sent Jesus, to die for our sins, and give eternal life to anyone who believes in him. When a person is saved, he is given eternal life, and is reconciled *back* into the family of God. Therefore, we are not in the family of God until we give our lives to Christ.

The devil thought he had destroyed man's ability to have eternal life, by bringing into the world death and sin. Not so! God sent Jesus to die for the sins of the world, and conquer death, and the power of the grave. Now eternal life is available to all who accept Jesus. Death, now, is only a stepping-stone into heaven, where we live forever with the Lord.

What shall we say about these things, and how does this relate to being considered a part of God's family? In the afore-mentioned scripture, Jesus referred to those who did the will of God, and obeyed the word of God, his family.

Those Jesus referred to, sat at his feet to learn his word, thereafter to obey it. How many in your family is doing that? How many are saved, and have the spirit of God in them? Those are the ones who have love in them. They have God's spirit, and are a part of God's family. We are born in sin, because of the disobedience of Adam and Eve. An unsaved status is not the intention of God. That's why he sent Jesus to *reconcile* us back to himself.

God doesn't force his will upon anyone, but is longsuffering that none will perish. God wants us all to be in his family. That's why he commissioned apostles, evangelists, prophets, pastor and teachers, to teach us. However, sharing the gospel can't be left to them. All of us must share the gospel with our own individual families, and with everyone else.

The benefits of a saved family are tremendous. No longer, will there be two families in one household, the saved and the unsaved. There will no longer be two different spirits, the spirit of the world, and the spirit of God. Hatred and enmity will no longer exist. There will be love, harmony, and unity in one spirit. There will only be peace and righteousness.

When I was young, I grew up next door to a family that had saved and unsaved members. My best friend was the young boy, who was about my age. We went to school together. His family was always fighting each other. If they weren't fighting over who would use the car, someone had stolen something from one of them. They would cut each other, shoot each other, lie on each other, and steal from each other. It was always the saved people who suffered most.

One of the traits of a person who lives in the flesh is covetousness. They always want more than they have. Usually, what they want belongs to someone else. It can be your money, your car, or your wife. Unsaved people have no boundaries, when it comes to covetousness. They will steal from their own mother. It doesn't matter to them. That's the character of human nature, the flesh. There's nothing good in it.

That's why so many family members are not speaking to one another. Thanksgiving dinner is, now, scarcely attended. Grudges are held, because family members can't forgive something that happened ten years ago. They don't come to family gatherings, because they can't stand to be around the person that hurt them. They remain bitter, angry, and filled with hatred. They refuse to forgive. That's the status of a lot of families, today.

Where there's love, however, none of the above problems exists. I'm not saying there won't be disagreements. There will! Anger may even come up, every now and then. Anger, in a saved person, will not escalate into a vendetta or grudge. Saved people are more apt to forgive than the unsaved. There is more peace, harmony, and unity when love is present in the family.

CHAPTER 4

EROS

The Greek word *Eros* is the word from which we get our word erotic. This word for love denotes intimacy, sex, and passion. This love is purely physical, but is the most popular form of love, today. Sex is in demand, and most people want it, without love. They do not want the emotional attachment. The physical pleasure derived therefrom seems to be sufficient, today.

It's not necessary to possess God's spirit to experience this love. A willing and available body is all you need. As a matter of fact, people are seemingly more willing to share genitalia with each other, than they are their hearts, with one another. Fornication and adultery are more accepted than love, today.

The popularity of this type of love doesn't mean God approves of it. By no means! Sex was intended for procreation in marriage. After all, it's the marriage bed that is undefiled (Hebrews 13: 4). Any other indulgence of sex is considered sin by God. Yet, most people prefer those indulgences.

God's intention is not void of pleasure. Sex is pleasurable in marriage also. The pleasure derived from sex in marriage has meaning, though. Outside of marriage, however, sex has no meaning. It's only used to please the flesh. The person isn't important, only their body, and the satisfaction derived therefrom.

Today, sex is used for many things. It's used in advertising. It's used to manipulate. It's used for blackmail. It's used for degradation. It's used for abuse. It's used for financial acquisition. It's used to create and promote careers. It's used for power. It's used for violence. It's used for pleasure. It's used in experiments. It's used in gender alterations. It's used to humiliate. It's used to slander. It's used in crime. It's used to express and enjoy pain. It's used for entertainment. Today, sex has gone to another level. Immorality does not seem a big enough word to adequately describe it.

There is a belief, in this world, that we own our bodies. People actually believe they have the right to give their bodies to whomever they want. What manufacturer doesn't own what he created? That should answer the question. Did you create yourself? If the answer is no, you don't own your body. God does! No one considers the God factor, though. Look at what the Word of God says about ownership. We don't own anything. God owns everything.

> "The earth is the Lord's, and the fullness thereof,
> the world, and they that dwell therein." (Psalm 24:1)

There's another scripture we should look at. I clearly speaks about fornication.

> "Now the body is not for fornication, but for the
> Lord; and the Lord for the body. And God hath
> both raised up the Lord, and will also raise up us
> by his own power. Know ye not that your bodies
> are the members of Christ? Shall I then take the
> members of Christ, and make them the members

of a harlot? What? Know ye not that he which joined to an harlot is one body? For two, saith he, shall be one flesh. But he that is joined unto the Lord is one spirit. Flee fornication. Every sin that a man doeth is without the body; but he that committeth Fornication sinneth against his own body. What? know ye not that your body is the temple of the Holy Ghost which is in you, which ye have of God, and ye are not our own? For ye are bought with a price: therefore glorify God in your body, and in your spirit, which are God's." (I Corinthians 6: 13-20)

There's a certain level of arrogance when it comes to exerting the individual will. We consider ourselves free. Therefore, we feel we have the right to do as we please. Do we? Obviously, people are not thinking about the above-mentioned scripture, when it comes to sex. If they were, they wouldn't commit fornication. Let's look at this scripture, anyway, and see how it may help people to stop fornicating.

The first thing pointed out in this text is that the body is for the Lord. It clearly states that God did not create the body for casual sex. The body was created to glorify God, and not to merely please ourselves. Let's face it! All of us have been there. In our younger years, and some in older years, we have put sex at the top of the list. I don't think any of us can be judgmental, because all of us have sinned, and come short of the glory of God. However, since I have been saved, I agree with the above scripture. I'm not saying I am perfect. I'm striving for it, because I believe the Word of God is true. Our bodies are for the Lord, to glorify him.

The reason people think fornication is harmless is, they think no one gets hurt. How can it be wrong, if two consenting adults agree to it? Well, let's examine that question, and see if fornication causes any harm, even when those participating have agreed to indulge themselves in it. Let's go to the Word of God.

The above-mentioned scripture says, "What? Know ye not that he which is joined to a harlot is one body? For two, saith he, shall be one flesh."

Few people realize that more than a pleasurable orgasm happens when two people have sex. In sex, two people are joined together, as one flesh. You become a part of the other person, without knowing it. It's almost like the consummation of marriage. There's no spiritual togetherness, because love is not present. There is, however, a joining together of the flesh. It causes you to remember that person. Your body remembers them, because you were joined together with them, during sex. This is exactly why a lot of people commit bigamy. They are never released from that fleshly union, before they marry someone else.

When you have that one-night stand, thinking you will never see that person again, you actually carry the memory of that person with you. It can be several years before you see that person. However, as soon as you do, your body remembers them. You remember the sex, and want to do it again, because you failed to divorce them, in order for both of you to be free.

The tragic thing is, many people end up committing adultery by resuming a sexual relationship with the person they never divorced. After years went by, since that one-night stand, they got married. They committed adultery, because they never got the one-night stand, out of their system. It was fornication when they were single. Now, that they're married, it's adultery.

The word of God says to "flee fornication." When you do it, you sin against your own body. The body is the mechanism God uses to get things done. We function for him, in order that his will be done in the earth. If others see you sinning, by committing fornication, you fail to glorify God, and you lose your witnessing power. Who will listen to you, then? How can you tell others about Jesus, when they see you doing the things they do? They'll call you a *hypocrite*. Only in obedience to God, will others recognize you to be a child of God.

The scripture (1 Corinthians 6: 13-20) we are still looking at says that you don't own your body. You've been bought with a price. Your body is the temple of the Holy Ghost, which lives inside of you. God wants to live in a clean place. Your body will not be clean if you choose to fornicate. If you will not live in a dirty house, how do you expect the Holy Ghost to do so? Don't grieve the spirit.

Remember in John 18: 36, when Jesus said, "My kingdom is not of this world?" The word kingdom signifies rulership. Jesus is saying here that his rulership is not of this world. The principles and guidelines of his way of living is not of this world. He is the ruler and law giver of his kingdom. People in Christ may live in the world, but they don't live by the principles of the world. They don't live in the flesh, as the world does. They live in the spirit. Therefore, fornication is not a way of life in the kingdom of God.

The world has sex whenever it desires to. There is no reverence for God. The world lives by the flesh, and desires to please only itself. Lust is selfish! Caring for others is not its method of operation. It has no future. Lust does not think about the future. It only seeks immediate gratification. Right here! Right now! Today! Now you see me. Now you don't. Maybe you will. Maybe you won't. That's the basic principle of lust. It's unreliable.

Lust is incapable of commitment. It wanders, seeking whom it may entice. Now, you know why so many people cheat, even when they're in a relationship. Don't think that a man is weak, because his woman cheated on him. That doesn't make him less than a man. That woman simply followed the desires of her flesh. She was the weak one. She couldn't control her flesh. She allowed her flesh to dominate her. Flesh wanders, and is incapable of commitment.

You've seen people get married, and in six months, they're divorced. They spend thousands of dollars for the ceremony, only to spend thousands more in divorce court. You know why? They got married for the flesh. God didn't join them together. They joined themselves together. When the bond is not of God, don't expect it to last.

The flesh has an insatiable appetite. It is never satisfied. When it gets hungry for something different, it will wander until it finds what it's looking for. The monotony and boredom of a single source of gratification, always sends the flesh looking for something new. Why? The flesh is incapable of loyalty. It's incapable of commitment. It is incapable of monogamy.

I don't know about you, but I was exactly like that. I had many girlfriends. When I got tired of one, I would move on to the next woman I could find. I would have my way with her until I got tired of her, too. I went looking for something new, as if sex with a different woman would make the difference. I was never happy. A different color of skin didn't bring me more joy. A more curvy body didn't make me happier. Bigger shapelier legs didn't appease me. Why? There was no love involved. There was nothing to touch the emptiness inside of me. And sex couldn't do it.

It doesn't matter how hard you try to find love through sex. It won't happen. How can a person get everlasting joy from a momentary pleasure? It's impossible! One thing I forgot to tell you. I was lonely and miserable. Even when I had sex with a different woman every weekend, it never brought me happiness. It only made me see how empty I really was.

I was lonely all the time. Sex with a lot of people doesn't make them your friends. They don't become valuable facets of your life. Friendships are not formed. You can't call on them in your time of trouble. They don't care about you like that. Sex is just pleasure, when love is absent. There is no meaning to it, and the only unity formed is in the body. Names are unimportant. Backgrounds are useless. Your income has no value, and what you drive has no significance. Only the body is important in Eros.

Individuals, who live by the flesh, have no morals. Don't expect them to do what's right. If they live in the flesh, they can't do what is right. They don't have that capacity. A person in the flesh will have sex with his sister's best friend, his wife's sister, his daughter's friend, his step-sister, and even his best friend's wife. There's nothing good in the flesh.

Those type of things cause corruption. People can get hurt or killed. Galatians 6: 8 says, "For he that soweth to his flesh shall of the flesh reap corruption; but he that soweth to the spirit shall of the spirit reap life everlasting."

Let me tell you a story. I once knew a lady who had a live-in boyfriend. She also had a fifteen year old daughter, who was blossoming into a curvaceous young lady. Well, the boyfriend was attracted to the young girl. He couldn't control his excitement, and eventually raped the young girl, while the mother was away at work.

The girl told her mother, but the mother didn't believe her daughter. Instead, the mother viciously reprimanded her. "You'd better stop telling lies. I had better not hear that you've mentioned this outside this house. You will be punished, and I will kick you out. You will not continue to stay here and cause trouble."

The young girl kept quiet. However, her anger and her bitterness intensified. She became a loner, because of the shame. She had no friends. By the time she was 18, and finished high school, while her mother was away from the house, she stabbed the live-in boyfriend 16 times, with a butcher's knife from the kitchen. He lost his life. She lost her freedom, and the mother lived with the guilt. All of that happened because of lust that couldn't be controlled.

Aspirations used to be to go to college, and get the job you always dreamed about. Now, many of the young ladies, today, dream about becoming famous. Some of them feel that if they go on the internet, and have sexual intercourse, or perform oral sex, they'll be successful. Why? They've seen other women do it, and they want what they have. They want the fame, and they want the money. I could name some of the women who have become successful that way, but I won't do that, even though it's public knowledge. You already know who the ladies are, who started out having sex on the internet, and got their own television shows.

Sex is big business. Ladies, today, are taking every advantage of that. You would think the young girls would be shame. No sir! They want to be known as the best, in whatever area of sexual immorality they are known for. They are getting naked for the camera as early as eighteen. To them, the money makes up for the shame, if there's any shame to begin with.

It seems as if looks are more important than substance, today. Women are more concerned about their appearances than what type of person they are. Emphasis seems to be placed on hair, nails, shoes, and clothes. The body and its shape are very important, too. Now, women look at their physical assets, and think how marketable they are.

Have you seen some of these music videos? Where is the emphasis placed? That's right! On the body. Women must have the talent to shake it, drop it, bounce it, and pop it. They call it "twerking." This talent began with the African-American community. The women knew their men liked that. So, they learned how to do it. Now, they can do it in different variations.

African-American women are not the only women who concentrate on this quality. Other races have joined this craze. African-American women no longer dominate this ability. Other women, from every other ethnic community, have incorporated this skill into their lives, to be sexy, or to be marketable.

You can see this craze everywhere, especially in dance clubs. Of course, it's in pornography, and the internet. Definitely, it is in the private bedroom. Women have found the secret that attracts men. What they attract, however, are men who just want sex. They don't attract love. They attract men who don't care if they know their names or not. Those men aren't there to get to know them. They only want their bodies. Believe it or not, women have accepted these arrangements. Being used doesn't seem to bother women anymore, and being respected doesn't seem to be high on their lists.

I don't have to tell you those affairs don't last. They don't! There's no commitment. Separation is easy. There's no pain at break-up. Why? There's no love! You only hurt when someone you love leaves you. There will be a problem, however, if you think the sex you had was love. Then, there will be emotional pain.

How many women believe sex is love? A lot! You know why? Because of the pleasure given to the body, and the attention they get. It has to be love. It feels too good not to be. Right? Wrong! Pleasure can be deceptive. Pleasure from sex alone only touches the body. That's as far as that pleasure goes. It doesn't fulfill the spirit, or the soul. After fornication is done, you are still empty. No matter how much sex you may have, it won't take away loneliness, depression, or emptiness.

Being chosen for having a sexy body doesn't mean you are appreciated. That, of course, is what most women want. It just doesn't happen. Many women think they are special, when someone wants to have sex with them. Such a woman has a shallow opinion of herself. When the body is the only area of attraction, you, as a person, are ignored. Your existence fails to be acknowledged.

Have you ever seen, in a movie, two people having sex the night before, but didn't know each other's name the next morning.

We know what their goal was. It wasn't to meet the love of their lives. They were just there for sex.

Have you ever had sex, and the person you were with never knew who you were? You were never asked where you were from. Your interests never came up. Your family structure was never a part of the conversation. Your goals and aspirations were never discussed. Not even your name came up. Only your body was important. How you felt was more important than whom you were.

When the body is the only connection, the union derived therefrom is short lived. So, do not equate multiple orgasms with love. Many women do. If you do, you will only get hurt. From that type of hurt, various behaviors can develop. Paranoia, suspicion, fear, distrust, revenge, and hatred, can all come from being manipulated and rejected.

When a person is rejected, they feel devalued. Their self-esteem is diminished, and they begin to have feelings of unworthiness. They feel useless, and unnecessary, like no one will ever love them again. Some people end up committing suicide. Some take drugs, trying to cover the pain. Some even become alcoholics, in an attempt to drown the hurt and shame. It's a bad feeling, knowing you have been deceived, and used like a commodity.

The deception in fornication is fulfillment. It promises to make you happy, but it doesn't have the power to deliver. Unlike true love, sex can't fulfill the mind, the heart, and the spirit. Love makes you know you belong. To what do you belong in fornication? You are forgotten when sex is finished. In love, you feel valued. In fornication, whatever enjoyment you get, it's temporary. All you get from fornication is a *false* sense of satisfaction. You can only get true fulfillment from love.

Some people get trapped in the flesh. You know how it is. You do something long enough, you become whatever you are doing. Fornication brings you down. You begin to think that you're only good enough for sex. Whenever someone is attracted to you, you automatically think they want sex, because that's all everybody else wanted.

Sex, then, becomes a lifestyle. Every time someone is attracted to you, you offer them sex, because that's all you've ever given. You begin to feel everyone wants the same thing from you. That's when you become trapped in that lifestyle. You not only relate to others that way, you will have become what you do. Then, you are referred to, and addressed by, insulting and degrading names. You answer to those names, because you accept that you are what you are called. Not only do men call you those names, you and your friends call each other those names. My God!

I'll tell you what happens after that. You miss out on love, because you become cynical towards love. Every person that offers you love is considered weak and foolish. You react in a cynical way, because you have accepted the way of the flesh as normal. Love is not normal, to a person who thinks she's just a body, meant to give pleasure to the opposite sex. That person lives a miserable life. No friends. No one relates to them like a real person. It's a life of loneliness. No one is interested in their well-being, how they are doing. They live a life of emptiness.

So many women have been abandoned, and left with children, by men who live a lifestyle of the flesh. Sex is all they wanted. They made babies, and they were never seen anymore. Our society is inundated with single parents, most of them women. Most often, these single women don't receive any financial help to raise these children. They end up not getting a husband. All they get is a *baby's daddy,* whom you never see until he wants more sex.

Have you ever seen that woman who is so promiscuous, she's not known by her name, only by her promiscuous activities, in the community? Everybody whispers about her, and talks about her behind her back. Nearly half the men in the community have had sex with her. Her reputation is a bad one, because of her sexual escapades. What the people don't understand about her is this: She only wants love in her life. She gives herself to men, hoping that one will want her enough to keep her, and love her. Unfortunately, she goes about it the wrong way, and she never gets what she wants. If she had only known what true love is, and where it comes from.

Some girls, who find themselves in that situation, go another route. They figure, since no one will like them for who they are, and all they want is sex, they might as well benefit financially from it. That's how some women become prostitutes, strippers, and escorts. Women like this do that for revenge. Making men pay is pay-back for the abuse they received. It's their way of robbing a man of his dignity.

It's really unfortunate that so many women have to resort to such a way of life. Just because men only want sex from you, doesn't mean you have no value. Stop believing what men say about you, or how they react to you. Believe what God says about you, not people. When God made you, He didn't make another person like you. You are unique. Psalms 139:19 says, "You are fearfully and wonderfully made." Only you have the character and the qualities that you possess. No one else!

No one can be you, or do the things you can do. You are special. You don't need to have sex, or take your clothes off, to be appreciated. Your body is not the entirety of your existence. You are more than a physical being. You are also a spiritual being, made in the image and likeness of Almighty God. Start loving yourself. Appreciate who God made you to be. Remember! When God made you, he didn't make a mistake.

Your body is the temple of the Holy Ghost. He wants to live in a clean place. So, take care of your body. Glorify God with your body. Don't let others abuse your body, by using it for their own pleasure, only to discard it whenever they've finished with it. Value who you are. "Don't be conformed to this world..." (Romans 12:2). Don't live by the principles of the world. Honor God, and obey him.

James 4:4 says, "Whoever is a friend of the world, is an enemy of God." You won't find love in someone who loves the world, or in someone who lives by the principles of the world. The world hates God, and the people of God. In the world, people have sex whenever they want, without any regard for God. They live by the flesh, and are separated from God. The way of fornication is death. Walk in the spirit, and you will have life eternal and peace.

My girlfriend and I, before I got saved, lived totally in the flesh. We thought we had it going on. We were so into each other. The problem with us was; we lived in denial. We wanted to believe we were happy, but we only communicated in bed. Sex was our primary mode of expression to one another. We didn't talk much. We refused to accept the fact that our only attraction toward each other was sex.

I got saved, and our relationship changed. I didn't want to just have sex anymore. I wanted a real relationship. I wanted to talk, cuddle, and give to her. She resented me! She wanted nothing to do with me. She hated me.

She couldn't be civil towards me. She insulted, and called me names. She even cursed God, and called him names. She hated my new way of life, and wanted no part of it. All she wanted was party and have sex. She knew nothing else, but she thought her way was the best way. Needless to say, I never saw her again. We parted ways. I left her to her clubs, drugs, and sex. I went on to serve the Lord.

A lot of girls, like my former girlfriend, go into adult films. Some are as young as 18 and 19 years old. There's no doubt they get the money. That's what it's all about for them. What about the shame and the humiliation? Do the men, who desire them, really appreciate them? It may look as if they don't care. They may not say anything about it, but they care. Some of the girls think the money they earn will help them gain respect. Some are even single mothers. What will their children say, when they find out what mommy did for a living?

What is going to happen, when they are tired of doing that sort of thing, or get too old to do it anymore? Will they be able to get married, or will every man they meet relate to them only on a sexual level? How will they react if the men they meet saw them stripping, or in a nude magazine pictorial? What if a man had all their DVD's? Will she ever be a real person to anyone, or will she always be considered a sex factory, used for the pleasures of men?

What will their children say? How will these mothers explain their sexual profession to their children? Will the children still respect them? What will the parent do, if the children decide to follow in her footsteps?

Children have a tendency to emulate what they see. You cannot tell them to do as I say, and not as I do. That won't work. Children imitate exactly what they see. Then, how difficult will discipline be? Will that parent be able to tell that child what, and what not, to do?

Proverbs 22:6 says, "Train up a child in the way he should go; and when he is old, he will not depart from it."

Training is more than lip service. You have to do more than talk to a child, if you want them to go in the right direction. Your talking must be corroborated by example. That child must see you practicing what you preach. So, if you tell your child not to have sex, and every night, a different man is sleeping over, what do you expect your child will do? After she comes to you and tells you she is pregnant, who do you think God will hold responsible?

I once knew a girl whose mother wanted her to be whore. The girl was extremely beautiful. She was full-figured, but she was like a magnet to men. They were drawn to her everywhere she went. She couldn't shake them off with a stick.

Her mother relentlessly preached the same sermon to her. "Those guys are always telling you how pretty you are. That's not going to put money in your pocket. What good is being beautiful, if you're broke? Having sex with them, just because you like them, won't get you paid. They'll get what they want, and leave you all alone. They may come back. They may not. Then, what will you have to show for giving your most precious possession away? You'd better wake up, and stop having sex for free." Well, the girl conceded, and became a whore at the age of 29. Remember what we said about making someone stumble? God said, "Woe unto him through whom offences come" (the one who causes one to stumble from what God had designed for them). That mother has a great deal to answer for.

According to Dr. Charles Stanley, "People live either by principles or preferences." Principles are biblical moral codes that, if you live by them, will benefit your life in a good way. On the other hand, people who live by preferences live by what they like, what they don't like, or what they desire."

People who live by principles, live with a single focus. Those who live by preferences, however, live lives that fluctuate. They don't adhere to any moral law. They live by their feelings. They can like something one minute. In the very next minute, they can be attracted to something, or someone else. They are extremely impulsive. They are also very unstable. They change like the wind. James 1: 8 says, "A double-minded man is unstable in all his ways." Would you want someone like that? No! Who wants a person with an unstable life?

Ladies, be cautious of those who live by preference. Just when you think you finally have the love of your life, they can see someone else they are attracted to. Suddenly, your number one status will have changed to number two, or three, or four.

You must always remember. The devil uses sex to make believers fall from grace. He does this to accuse the believer before God. He does everything he can to discredit the believer. He figures, if he can discredit us, he destroys our witnessing power. Then, we are unable to tell anybody about Jesus Christ. After all, who will listen to a fornicator, right? He's famous for doing this to teachers, preachers, and pastors. Any Christian is fair game, though. "He roams to and fro, seeking whom he may devour" (I Peter 5:8).

Another thing the devil uses sex for is to slander the name of the believer. In so doing, he ruins the reputation of the believer, and destroys his integrity, and his dignity. He knows that if he can produce shame and humiliation, the believer may lose his self-esteem. His self-worth will go down. When that happens, the believer will begin to doubt himself, and begin to doubt God.

When faith is low, the devil knows the believer will lose interest in the things of God. Instead of going to church, he will go to the club. Instead of getting high on the Holy Ghost, he will get high on drugs and alcohol. Instead of being faithful to just one woman, fornication and adultery will become a new lifestyle. Instead of reading the Word of God, it is replaced with pornographic DVD's. Oh, the destruction sex can bring into a person's life. It can knock down the strongest man, if you let it. Ask Solomon!

Sex is destructive. It can't produce happiness, by itself. I am sure a lot of people think they are happy, because sex feels so good. That's all a part of the devil's deception. That good feeling lures you into bondage. Oh yeah! You are in bondage, if you live by the flesh. Sex is not an upward staircase. No! It is, rather, a downward spiral of destruction, without love. Seek love, and sex will have more meaning.

Now, this is what shocks me. The women today seem to have no self-esteem. They are exploited, and they like it. They don't love themselves, and they don't have any self- respect. The woman, who loves herself, won't let someone treat her badly, or address her by using obscene names. The women of today have accepted this type of treatment as normal. To be treated with respect and love is unacceptable, now. Only wimps treat women like that, they say. Did I miss something? Isn't that backward? I thought it was the other way around.

The woman, who lives this type of lifestyle, lives in a fantasy world. She has deceived herself into thinking she is more appreciated than other women, because men chase her. Men pay money to see her nude, or to have sex with her. She thinks she is special, because men prefer her more than other women. Her degradation is viewed as fame and popularity. She really thinks she is important, even though she is only an exploited commodity. What a stronghold sex has weaved, in the minds of so many young women, today.

Love is the only fulfillment. Sex is temporary. Love is everlasting. You choose.

CHAPTER 5

PHILEO

The Greek meaning of the word "Phileo" is brotherly love, or friendship. Do not confuse this brotherly love with the household of faith. This love is not that type of love. Neither does it have that type of unity. Brotherly love, in the household of faith, is contingent upon everyone possessing the Holy Ghost. The brotherly love described here is strictly among people who are attached to one another, because they like one another. They merely consider themselves *friends*.

I know you will agree with me, when I say, the word friend is a word that is tossed around freely, and insincerely. What is a true friend? Every so-called friend I have ever had was only my friend, when things were in their favor. When things were bad, they terminated the friendship, and I would never see them again. One thing I do know is this: A true friend is someone you can trust. It's someone who really loves you, and on whom you can rely. You can confide in a true friend, and he won't spread your personal business abroad.

Jesus said in John 15:13, "Greater love hath no man than this, that a man lay down his life for his friends." Do you have a friend like that? I certainly don't have a friend like that. I could barely get someone to cover for me at work, let alone, die for me. That's a mighty strong bond, for someone to value you so much, they are willing to die for you. I have never been that close to anyone. Neither have I ever had a friend, who felt like that toward me.

One thing I know about Jesus is that he didn't just talk love. He demonstrated it. Remember when I told you love is action? Love is more than what you say. Love is what you do. People are not like that, today. No one will put themselves in jeopardy, especially for someone who isn't related to them. Oh sure! They may talk like they would, but when it is time to put those words into action, they mysteriously slip away.

Have you ever been betrayed by someone who declared they were your friend? What did they do? Sleep with your girlfriend? Steal you promotion? Slander your name, in order to discredit you? Or did they steal a sizable amount of money from you? The word that has replaced friendship, I think, is self-preservation. You can't rely on someone else, when they're thinking only of themselves.

Jerry Springer got rich on sso-called friends betraying each other. Lust and covetousness seem to override friendship. It's not Mr. Springer's fault. What's so bad about that type of betrayal is, the betraying party continues to deceive the other person by pretending to still be their friend. They continue to eat together, go together, and hang together, until the betrayal is discovered. Then, that used-to-be friend is never seen again.

In John 15: 15, Jesus says, "Henceforth, I call you not servants; for the servant knoweth not what the lord of the house doeth: but I have called you friends; For all things that I have heard of my Father I have made known to you."

The word for servant is *"slave."* Jesus is saying that, no longer, will his disciples be called slaves. A slave is not privy to what the master knows. He merely follows orders, and does what the master tells him to do. In the future, they would be called friends. They were, now, people he could trust, and confide in. Not that Jesus needed help from them. He was, now, willing to trust them with things the Father told him. Things nobody else knew.

Do you have any friends like that? Got anybody you can really trust with your secrets? How many times have you told secrets to someone you thought was your friend? You confided in them, trusted them not to tell anyone else. Just the opposite happened, though. They took that information, and propagated it. They told everyone they could. Even other friends began to shun you because of what they heard. Everyone turned his back on you, and stopped talking to you. The tragic aspect about this type of thing is this: People believe gossip and rumors, without knowing if the information is true.

What would a true friend do? Wouldn't a true friend go to his friend and warn him about the fallout that's threatening to damage him? Look at what Jesus did, when he knew the devil was after one of his disciples.

> "And the Lord said, Simon, Simon, behold, Satan hath desired to have you, that he may sift you like wheat: But I have prayed for thee, that your faith fail not. And when thou art converted, strengthen thy brethren." (Luke 22: 31-32)

Why don't we have friends like that? Today, the most popular response is, "That's none of my business. I'm not going to get involved." Therefore, that so-called friend remains silent, and lets his friend get hurt, when he could have warned him. He chose to protect himself, rather than help protect his friend. I don't know about you, but I don't want a friend like that. I want a friend who really loves me, and cares if I get hurt.

How many times have you seen a person's friend get robbed? What happened? When the authorities came around to investigate the robbery, no one would say anything, including the friend. He was the closest one to the victim, but because he decided not to get involved, he let the robbers go free. What type of friend is that?

Before they received the Holy Ghost, the disciples of Jesus did the same thing. They looked out for themselves, too, when they thought their lives were in danger. When Jesus was on his way to the cross, all of his disciples turned their backs on him. When Jesus was feeding five thousand, with two fishes and five barley loaves, healing the sick, and raising people from the dead, the disciples were with him. However, when they thought their lives were in jeopardy, they sought to protect themselves. Peter even denied knowing Jesus 3 times (Matthew 26: 69-75). After the day of Pentecost, and the disciples received the Holy Ghost, their love and loyalty never wavered. All of them loved Jesus, even unto death. It took the Holy Spirit to enable the disciples to love Jesus, as he loved them.

We aren't any different. We also need the Holy Spirit to enable us to love our friends the way we should. If a person says he's your friend, and doesn't have the Holy Ghost, there are many temptations that can make him betray you. Money, sex, power, position, envy, jealousy, and image, are all things that can easily make a so-called friend turn on you. Don't be surprised when it happens.

Without the Holy Ghost, a person cannot resist the devil. The devil is too strong to fight, in your natural state. Look at what the word of God says about that.

> "For though we walk in the flesh, we do not war after the flesh: (For the weapons of our warfare are not carnal, but mighty through God to the pulling down of strong holds;) Casting down

imaginations, and every high thing that exalted itself against the knowledge of God, and bringing into captivity every thought to the obedience of Christ. (II Cor. 10: 3-5)

If your friends are not equipped with the tools of warfare, they are susceptible to being influenced by the devil. Pick your friends wisely. Not everyone is capable of loving the way a true friend should. Jesus had a friend like that. His friend betrayed him, too. This so-called friend was tempted by the devil, to betray Jesus. Satan used money to make him yield. Look at what the word of God says about him. His name was Judas.

"Then entered Satan into Judas surnamed Iscariot, being of the number of the twelve. And he went his way, and communed with the chief priests and captains, how he might betray him unto them. And they were glad, and covenanted to give him money. And he promised, and sought opportunity to betray him unto them in the absence of the multitude." (Luke 22: 3-6)

Judas wore a mask. He pretended to be one thing, when in fact, he was another. He had his own agenda. He went along with everything, until he couldn't do it any longer. Remember, when I said, what's inside, will come out? Good or bad, it will come out.

You can't pretend to love someone. It's impossible for the flesh to imitate the spiritual. Human nature can't emulate God. God has to be in you, for others to see him in you. When God is in you, love is in you. There's no need to pretend. Real love will manifest itself. Ditch the pretenders! Who needs them? Brotherly love is a valuable thing. Don't waste your time with pretentious people.

One thing you can't do is buy friendship. The more you do for someone, the more they want you to do. You can't buy love, and you can't buy acceptance. When you, no longer, can do the things they like, they will discard you, and cease to be your friend. Don't let people use you.

A real friend accepts you the way you are. He doesn't try to change you into who he wants you to be. He doesn't take from you, and he doesn't require you to constantly prove you are his friend. He doesn't associate with you to get what he can, and then leaves you after he has gotten what he wanted. A real friend doesn't manipulate, exploit, or deceive you. A true friend is honest. A real friend doesn't care if you are rich or poor. He loves you for who you are.

Jesus said, "Thou shall love thou neighbor as thyself" (Matthew 19: 19). This verse is the epitome of brotherly love. This verse is not just directed to those you know, or to just who lives in your neighborhood. This applies to everyone. Everyone is your neighbor. Not just the person next door, your coworkers, those with the same color of skin as you, or your classmates. You are to love all people, whether you know them or not.

In this society, empathy is a lost emotion. A person can be lying on a sidewalk, hurt, and no one will stop to help. They do not want to get involved. People are afraid. If the shoe were on the other foot, and they were lying there, it would upset them if no one stopped to help. Why is it we want love extended to us, but will not extend love to others? That's such a selfish attitude. That's not brotherly love.

There are so many people living next door to someone, and even though they may have lived there 10 years, they have not met their neighbor. Why are people so afraid? Everyone lives in a protective shell. People don't even speak anymore. Come on! What does it cost just to say hello to someone?

Can you see why our society is so fragmented? We are so divided, because we are afraid to love each other. We live with so many suspicions. We assume if we trust someone, we will be taken advantage of. Sure! There's a risk in the unknown. You never know, however, how someone will treat you, unless you step out on faith. It takes faith to love. Do not assume ahead of time what the outcome will be. That would be too judgmental. Take the risk, and trust God.

The best example of brotherly love, and true friendship, is the story of Jonathan and David. In 1 Samuel 18:3, it is stated that "Jonathan loved David as he loved his own soul." That simply means he loved David like he loved himself. Even though Saul, Jonathan's father, hated David and wanted to kill him, Jonathan stood by David's side as a friend, and a brother.

Jonathan did something unusual. Often, when the father hates, or dislikes someone, the entire family does the same. Jonathan didn't allow the evil influences of this father to persuade him. He followed his own heart and mind.

Have you ever seen a clique that demands everyone, in it, to hate another person, because the leader of the clique hates them? Then, if you don't do it, you are kicked out of the clique. The clique, in turn, tries to ruin your reputation by spreading lies on you. That certainly isn't brotherly love. As a matter of fact, the Word of God has something to say about that. Look at this!

> "We know we have passed from death unto life, because we love the brethren. He that loveth not his brother abideth in death. Whosoever hateth his brother is a murderer: and ye know that no murderer hath eternal life abiding in him." (1 John 3: 14-15)

When you hate your brother, the Bible says, "You're a murderer." Now, we all are familiar with the physical aspects of murder. But there is another way to murder a person. That's with the tongue. That evil, and uncontrollable, thing in our mouths has the power to kill character, dignity, integrity, and relationships. It can bring the strongest man down. The tongue can destroy a family, a marriage, even a business. "It is an unruly evil, full of deadly poison" (James 3:8).

Another thing I have seen among so-called friends is covetousness. Why does one friend always sleep with his best friend's girl, or wife? Why do we want what doesn't belong to us? Are we really that greedy? Your best friend and your girlfriend are two people you trust. When both of them betray you, it hurts. That's a hurt you don't get over quickly.

Covetousness is not only greed, it's also idolatry. Idolatry, in this sense, is "*image worship.*" When your friend covets your wife, he has an image, in his mind, of him and your wife together. That's where sin begins, in the mind. Every action begins with a thought.

The sex act doesn't have to be physically committed, for sin to have taken place. Jesus says, "Whosoever looketh on a woman to lust after her hath committed adultery with her already in his heart" (Matthew 5: 28). In other words, when the fantasy takes place in the mind, sin takes place. It's as if you've already committed adultery, without actually committing adultery.

I had this friend, who didn't come by my house that often. However, when I got a new girlfriend, he would drop by whenever the game was on, or just to hang out. Every Saturday, there he was. I thought we were getting closer, like brothers, until my girlfriend told me he made a play for her. Of course, after I confronted him, he never came around again.

True brotherly love exists when each party possesses the Holy Ghost. That's when two people have fellowship with one another. They're joined together in the Spirit. Without the Holy Spirit, there can be no true unity. If someone, who doesn't have the Holy Spirit, is hanging around you, and you can't figure out why, there may be an ulterior motive for doing so. Only those, who are born of God, can be true friends.

That's why, in the church, people refer to one another as brother and sister. Each believer has been born into one family, the family of God. Therefore, love is shared from heart to heart.

Brotherhood is formed, not just in immediate environments, but throughout the world. There's love for those in other countries, even though we haven't met. We aren't jealous of one another. We don't covet each other's belongings. We support one another, and desire for each other the highest good.

Then why, I ask myself, are we so divided? So many things separate us. Denominational differences is one of the walls that doesn't seem to come down. When will we accept the fact that there's only "One Lord; One Faith; and One Baptism?" (Ephesians 4:5). There will not be a Baptist section in heaven. Neither will there be a Methodist, a Pentecostal, or a Catholic section in heaven. So, why are we in sections down here? Where is the brotherly love? Where is the unity?

Hermeneutical and theological differences have plagued us also. For some reason, we cannot agree on the interpretation of certain things in God's word. So, we consider those who do not believe what we believe, not to be our brothers.

Some say you must be baptized in the name of Jesus only. Some say, unless you are baptized in the Holy Ghost, with the evidence of speaking in tongues, you are not saved. Some say God did not call women to preach. Then, you have pre-millenniums, post-millenniums, and the a-millenniums. I could go on and on, with the disagreements that keep us a part. Those are just some of the things that keep brotherly love from prospering.

It's not skin color that makes us brothers, either. It's the spirit inside. We are spirits, housed inside a physical body. What's more important, how a person looks, or who a person is? I think that perspective is somewhat shallow. It stops brotherly love from flourishing. If we continue to judge a person based on how he looks, we will miss the opportunity of actually knowing who that person is. There's more to a person than skin color. Come on! The sixties are long gone.

We, who are of the household of faith, have a job to do. It's imperative that brotherly love spreads. The world has to see the love of God in us, and it has to be shared. In John 13:35, Jesus said, "By this shall all men know you are my disciples, if you have love one to another." All we have to do is love one another, and let the world see that we love one another. When they see the awesome love of God, they will want what we have—the Spirit of the living God.

Strive for brotherly love.

CHAPTER 6

AGAPE

Agape love is the *godly* kind of love. It's the way God loves us. It's unconditional. He loves us in spite of, not because of. In spite of all our imperfections and faults, God still loves us. He doesn't love us because he needs us to do something for him. God isn't trying to get something from us. He loves us because He can't help it. It's his nature to love. He is love. (I John 4:8).

The love a person has for you, should be unconditional. They, too, should love you in spite of, and not because of. When they fell in love with you, they didn't fall in love with a perfect person. They must accept your strong points, as well as your not-so-strong points.

God loves us when we lie to him, when we fornicate, or when we commit adultery. He loves us when we stray, when we are rebellious, when we are unforgiving, when we disobey, and even when we fail him. He loves us in spite of our shortcomings. He doesn't love the sins we commit, but he loves us. Our sins still must be paid for, but even his chastening is love (Hebrews 12:6).

Have you ever been loved by someone, you didn't know existed? That's how God loved us. He loved us before we even knew him. Even when we were the unlovely, and the unlovable, God exhibited his love for us. Romans 5:8 says, "But God commendeth his love toward us, in that, while we were yet sinners, Christ died for us."

God didn't just say he loved us. He illustrated his love. He didn't wait until we believed in him. Neither did he wait for us to give our lives to him. Instead, while we were still sinners, he gave his only Son, to die on a cross for our sins.

That's what's wrong with a lot of people, today. They can't love you until you meet their standards. You have to be like this, act like that, talk like those, and dress like them. You have to drive a certain type of car, live in a certain type of house, live in a certain zip code, and make a certain amount of money. If you fall short of those standards, you are not eligible for their love. That isn't loving *"in spite of."* That's loving *"because of."*

There were no strings attached to God's love. He didn't look for anything in return, for giving his only Son, to die on a cross. No! God didn't say, "Look! I'm going to give my only Son to die for you, and eliminate the penalty of sin (death) from you. All you have to do is give your life to me, serve me, and worship me." There were no negotiations, and no conditional requirements. He just gave his love, because he wanted us to have it. No strings attached.

Have you ever been placed under obligation, just to be loved by someone? What about the old classic? "If you love me, you would have sex with me." Remember that one? What about this one? "If you love me, you'll co-sign for me to get that car. You know I wouldn't do anything to get you in trouble." Then, as soon as you keep your end of the bargain, they miss a payment, and you are left holding the bag.

If you have to pay for love, or do something drastic for it, that's not love. Love is free! There are no strings attached to true love, and proof of love is not necessary. Love proves itself.

Love has to give. It can't help it, because giving is a part of love's nature. It seeks to satisfy the other person. If someone says they love you, and never gives, you may want to reevaluate that relationship.

The person who never gives, but is always on the receiving end, isn't really in love with you. He doesn't care that much about the relationship. He merely cares about what the relationship can do for him. Giving shows appreciation. It shows that you care.

It's unfortunate that giving is not well received, today. In a society where "*game*" is so popular, giving is looked upon as a weak trait of character. Even though giving is what love does, men are not supposed to give. They should have enough game to make the woman give, because giving is an act of *submission,* according to the world perspective. When a man gives too quickly, the woman will assume she made him submit to her. Consequently, she will lose respect for him, because giving signifies *surrender.* She doesn't want him to surrender to her. She wants him to make her surrender to him. She doesn't want to dominate. She wants to be dominated. That's the way of the world.

Make no mistake about it! Even though the woman has no respect for the man, she will still keep the gifts he gave her. They give credibility to her game. However, she won't give her heart to him, because, to her, he showed weakness, by showing love.

Let me get this straight. If you show love, you are considered a loser. If you don't have the skills of deception (game), enough to make a woman surrender to you, you are weak. I see. I have to be able to dominate a woman's mind with lies and deception, in order to make her surrender to me. If I show love and kindness, I will lose my credibility as a man also. How stupid is that? Is that where the phrase, "*Good guys finish last,*" comes from? That's not what the Bible says. Mark 10:31 says, "Many that are first shall be last; and the last first."

If that's the way of this world, it appears that women like being treated like trash. That's really unfortunate. A man has to be ruthless, and apathetic. He can't show his feelings. He isn't a man, if he does. The only one that should show love is the woman. How crazy is that? God wants men to give love, and receive love, too. He has no respect of persons. He isn't more partial to one gender, more than he is to the other. What he wants for women, he wants for men, also.

To all the men who choose not to love, because you feel it makes you look weak, forget that! The weakness is not in loving. The weakness is in not loving. Remember! Whoever loves, has the presence of God in them. Ignore the haters, who say you are weak because you choose to love. Love, and keep giving to the one you love.

Giving is not always monetary. Other things like your time, your affection, your counsel, your protection, and your provision, are all things that can be beneficial to the person you love.

Giving is sacrificial. You don't check your inventory, to see what will be left for you, before you give. "Man! I'm not going to have enough left to go to the concert, if I give this $100. I'll just give 25. That way, I can kill two birds with one stone." Did God look at his inventory, before he gave his Son? No! He already knew he had only one Son. Our need was more important than his inventory. He was willing to sacrifice.

Does the person who loves you look at his inventory, before he gives to you? Does he make sure he has enough left for himself, before he meets the need that's important to you? "Sweetheart, I would love to help you with your daughter, but I've got to get my car repaired. If I didn't have to do that, I would definitely help you get that medication for her." Sound familiar? That's not love. Love doesn't put itself before the need of the person loved.

Suppose you fall in love with someone who is poor? Your love for that person should help their life improve. Suppose your loved one is depressed? Love should bring a new joy into that person's life. What if your loved one has been abused before? Your love ought to lift them to a new level of appreciation, and bring about a higher degree of self-esteem. What if your loved one has trouble trusting? Your love should help them trust again. Whatever the need, love has the power to meet it. Love should enhance, and improve the existence of the other person.

Everyone can't love like that. It takes the Holy Spirit to love like that. No one can love in his own power. That's a truth people have refused to accept. There are people who believe they don't need God. They continue to try things, on their own. The results are not what they had in mind. They go from one relationship to another, never finding what they are looking for. That leaves them lonely and miserable. You can't have your cake and eat it, too. You can't have love without God.

I do not know about you, but I've known that misery. I totally ignored God. I went after what I wanted. I thought I knew what was best for me. I thought I knew what love was. I found out, I didn't know anything. I knew just enough to get my heart broken.

In the first place, I picked the woman. My choice was based on beauty. I was always partial to the full-figured woman. So, I thought I had the right woman, because she fit the physical dimensions I liked. She had a pretty face. She wore a size 12 or 14, and had beautiful curves. She had high arches in her feet, and her legs looked good in high heel shoes.

I forgot she had a spirit, the wrong spirit. I got lost in the physical. I neglected to see the most important thing. I was in lust, not in love. I loved her body. I paid no attention to her spirit. Totally ignoring the person, I was mesmerized by beauty.

I found out later she was the wrong woman. Her outside beauty was impeccable, but she didn't know God. Love wasn't present. Beauty may have gotten my attention, but I soon discovered she lived in the flesh, not in the spirit. That ended in a heart-breaking experience. I focused on the wrong thing, and even though I learned a lot from it, I paid a pretty price. What was my lesson? Never equate beauty with goodness.

Agape also has beauty. You can't see it at first. It's slowly revealed, as you interact with it.

This type of love is so unusual; your perception of it will transcend your own comprehension.

It's so beautiful how love cares for you before you even know it exists.

There's a beauty in the way love chooses you, without making you adhere to a certain set of standards.

It's so beautiful how love gives, when you don't deserve it. There's a beauty in how it keeps caring, even when it has been wronged.

I cherish how love never leaves you, how it stays by your side, even in the most horrendous situations.

It's wonderful how love takes the initiative to meet your need, even before complaints of pain, sorrow, or lack, are made.

I love how love changes you, and you begin to look, feel, and act like love. You begin to embody the love given to you. You literally become a portrait of love.

I like the way love lifts my self-esteem, and makes me feel important. I know I belong, when love is present. I'm not just some misfit, who doesn't know who he is, or where he fits in.

Love makes me like myself. I respect myself. I have no notions to self-destruct. Love makes me know I have value. I feel needed, and wanted. Love makes me want to stay around to receive all that it has to offer, because I like being in the presence of love.

There's a certain type of security in love. You feel safe, in its presence. You know there is no danger, and that no hurt or harm, will come to you.

Love comforts me when I am low in spirit. Depression can't live here, when love is present. Love gives me joy, a joy that is incomprehensible. Even in turmoil, I have joy.

Self-pity is something that has become obsolete. I am not pessimistic. I am positive, and I love being who love has created. The new me is who I share with others, because I want them to know love also. I want them to see and feel the transforming quality of love.

I don't walk in darkness anymore. I walk in the light of love. Love leads me. Love guides me. Love protects me from the reproaches of the world. It covers many of my mistakes, and helps me maintain my dignity, and my integrity.

I know it sounds as if I think I am perfect, and have no flaws. I assure you, I am far from being perfect. I have so many flaws, I can't count them all. It isn't I, who is perfect. It's love that's perfect. Love is the one who has no flaws. My imperfections make me see my need for love.

Without love, I tend to stray away from the path of righteousness. Love makes me do right.

I have done so many wrong things. I have forsakened love. I have mistreated love. I have abused love. I have ignored love. I have tried to manipulate love. I have lied to love. I have cheated on love. I have betrayed love. I have run from love. Thank God love is filled with forgiveness and mercy

It saddens me that love is not well received. Instead of seeking good, evil is what people want. People don't accept love, because they refuse to accept God. Things of the devil are more preferred, today. Lies are accepted more than the truth. Evil is called good, and good is called evil. Humiliation is preferred. Degradation is considered a form of affection. Shame is looked upon as fame and popularity, and lasciviousness is considered a work of art.

Momentary pleasure is preferred to everlasting joy. People seemingly accept momentary bliss, because maybe they don't believe everlasting joy exists. On the other hand, maybe they think they don't deserve love. Perhaps, they think love is unreachable.

Love is the life-line to joy. There is no joy without it. People may act as if they have joy and peace. Unless love is in their lives, they are only deceiving themselves. You may have money. You may have houses and land. You may have fame and popularity. Without love, none of those things will profit you anything. Love is the greatest treasure. Love is the greatest gift.

CHAPTER 7

LOVE AND MARRIAGE

There are many reasons to get married. The best reason, however, is love. Love, is the main ingredient of marriage. Without this ingredient, the marriage is doomed from the beginning. That means that, not only is God not in the marriage, love isn't in the marriage either. No wonder so many marriages end in divorce.

Marrying for sex will not insure longevity. What if your spouse gets ill, and can't have sex anymore? Will you still love them, or will you seek a healthier spouse, that is able to give you the sex you desire?

Some people marry for money. They do so because they think they will find financial security. What if your money is met with financial disaster, and is depleted in the twinkling of an eye? Will you seek a richer spouse, who can give you the financial security you crave?

A lot of people marry for image and power. They want all of their friends to envy them for whom they are, or for whom they married. They live in a mansion on the hill. They're rich, and have all of life's amenities. They wear the finest clothes, and adorn their bodies with the most expensive jewelry. What would happen if your spouse lost the clout, the influence, and the power? Would you seek another spouse who could give you the image you are accustom to having?

I'm not saying there is anything wrong with wanting good sex in your marriage. I'm not saying it is wrong to have financial security in marriage. I'm not even saying that having a good image is wrong. I'm only saying that, without love, all of the above profits you nothing. Love should be the sole objective for marriage. When love is present, everything else will fall in place.

If a person really wants love, his first desire should be salvation. Only the saved person has love inside, because only the saved person has the spirit of God. Listen at what the word of God says. We have mentioned this text before, but it's worth mentioning again.

Remember what I John 4:7-8 says? We talked about this earlier. "...love is of God; and everyone that loves is born of God, and knows God. He that loves not knows not God: for God is love."

What does that mean? That means, if you want love in your life, you will only find it in a believer. Only those, who have accepted Jesus as Lord and Savior, have love.

An unbeliever cannot receive love, because only a believer can receive, from God, the things of God. Therefore, the best way, to receive true love, is to get saved. Then, the spirit of God will reside in you. Only, then, will you abide in love, and love will abide in you.

When two people get married, they are joined together by God. That means they are joined together by love. They aren't joined together because they wanted each other so badly. No! They are joined together because both are whom God wanted for each of them. Oh! I'm sorry. I thought you knew that, when two people are joined together in love, it's God who does the choosing, and it's God who does the drawing. That's why, at wedding ceremonies, the preacher says, *"What God has joined together, let no man put asunder."*

It's always better if God picks your spouse. We tend to "look on the outside appearance, while God looks at the heart" (1st Samuel 16:7). Our evaluations of another person are superficial, because we can only see the exterior of a person. We see how beautiful they are, how shapely they are, how rich they are, how educated they are, and how resourceful they are.

God, on the other hand, can see a little deeper. He can see inside a person. He can see the heart. We can't! The outside of a person doesn't tell who a person is, just how that person looks. This can be deceiving, because people can put up various facades. They can make you think they are one person when, in fact, they are actually someone else. Sometimes, you don't discover who a person really is until you live with them, even if then.

I had a friend who made that mistake. For the sake of explanation, I'll call him Sam. Sam's idea of the perfect woman was a pretty face, nice figure, and shapely legs. In his search for a wife, he found the woman that had what he desired. She had all the physical qualities Sam loved. He popped the question, and she accepted. They got married.

Sam was saved, and was a regular church goer. His wife was not saved, but Sam didn't know that. He assumed she was saved, because she always went to church with him. They never discussed the spiritual side of their lives, because Sam was too mesmerized by her outward appearance.

In the beginning of the marriage, Sam's wife was spiritually cooperative. She never complained about Sam going to church during the week, like to Bible study on Wednesdays. As a matter of fact, she even sang in the choir. She didn't go to church on Wednesdays, but she did go on Thursdays. Everything seemed good, on the surface. Things changed, however, when Sam was called into the ministry.

Sam prepared himself for ministry, and went to seminary. Two years, after graduation, he was called to pastor his first church. His wife never supported him in the ministry. She never attended Sam's church. She stayed at the church they attended, before Sam's call to pastor. Needless to say, the marriage ended in divorce.

This divorce was Sam's fault. Had he let God pick his wife for him, instead of picking her himself, the results would have been better. First, he picked her based on her outward beauty. That means Sam chose her according to the flesh. He never considered who the woman was, and never really met her. He was more interested in how she looked. "Lust of the eyes is of the world, not of the spirit" (1ˢᵗJohn 2:16). Sam's desire got the best of him. He may have been saved, but he allowed his flesh to override the spirit.

Secondly, he assumed that because she went to church, and sang in the choir, she was saved. People aren't saved because they go to church. It's just the opposite. People go to church, because they are saved. Saved people aren't just in the church. The church is in them. Listen at what the word of God says about that. "Not everyone that says unto me, Lord, Lord, shall enter into the kingdom of heaven; but he that does the will of my Father which is in heaven" (Matthew 7:21).

The church is filled with people who merely go through the rituals of the church. They think, because they pay tithes, participate in communion, have been baptized, sing in the choir, and serve on the usher board, or the deacon board, they are saved, and are going to heaven. If you aren't careful, you can fall into the same trap as Sam, looking at things from the outside. Remember? He thought he married someone with the Holy Spirit. All he got was a wolf in sheep clothing. Don't let the outward appearance fool you. It can cause you a lot of disappointment and heartache.

Once you have become a believer, marry another believer. Don't marry an unbeliever, and be unequally yoked. The unbeliever doesn't have the Holy Ghost. Therefore, love is not present in them. Marriage to them will be one-sided. By that I mean, you will be the only one who possesses love. Now, answer this question for me. How can one give love, when he doesn't have it?

Remember 1 John 4:16? "...God is love; and he that dwells in love dwells in God, and God in him." How many times do I have to say this? I'll keep saying it, if it'll keep someone from being unequally yoked. That's a relationship that only ends in hurt, pain, and disappointment. Only believers have love to give each other. Why? They have God in them. If you have love, you have God. If you have God, you have love. That's it. That's all! The unbeliever has neither.

Do you remember the old western movies? Remember the two oxen pulling the cart? Well, the wooden thing on their necks was a yoke. It was used by the driver to guide the oxen in the same direction.

The yoke was usually made out of wood. The dimensions of the yoke had to be exact, to fit the necks of the oxen. It had to be even, in order for the oxen to move *side-by-side*. If the dimensions were too small for the necks of the oxen, moving was very abrasive, and would cause pain and injury to the oxen.

Also, if the yoke was uneven, the oxen would move unevenly. One would be in front, and the other one would be behind. They would move, but not side-by-side. Any effort to get side-by-side would hurt the oxen, because the unbalanced yoke didn't allow them to move evenly. Whenever it was necessary for the oxen to increase their speed, the pain and injury would intensify.

Let's look at the Word of God, and see how this illustration of a yoke compares to the marriage of a believer, to an unbeliever. Let's see why God advises us against this type of marriage.

> "Be ye not unequally yoked together with
> unbelievers: for what fellowship has righteousness
> with unrighteousness? and what communion has
> light with darkness? (II Corinthians 6: 14)

The first thing this text says is "be ye not unequally yoked together with unbelievers." Of course, this statement is directed to believers. It's only saying not to associate discordantly. The unbeliever does not have the spirit of love, and is incapable of giving or receiving love. The believer, on the other hand, does have the spirit of love. The believer is born of God, and knows God. The unbeliever is not born of God, and does not know God. Therefore, there is no commonality between the two.

If you put several cubes of ice in a glass of water, the association is harmonious. Why? Both elements have something in common. Ice is harder than water, but it is the same as water. Ice is only frozen water. The association, therefore, is not a discordant one. It is a harmonious one, because both elements have the same ingredients. They are yoked together equally, not unequally.

"What fellowship does righteousness have with unrighteousness?" In other words, what "participation" does doing right have with doing wrong? When wrong is implemented, right isn't in participation. When you see wrong, you won't find right. The two have nothing in common, just as the believer has nothing in common with the unbeliever.

Unbelievers are not only in the world, they are of the world. They don't just live in the world, they live by the principles of the world. What principles? Let's look at the Word of God, and see.

> "For all that is in the world, the lust of the flesh,
> and the lust of the eyes, and the pride of life, is not
> of the Father, but is of the world." (I John 2:16)

These three things are the principles the world lives by. Lust of the flesh [sexual immorality], lust of the eyes [greed], and the pride of life [idolatry]. Contrary to how the world lives, the believer lives by the word of God. Those who are trying to live right, do not *participate* in activities that are wrong, and that are against the word of God. Doing right has no fellowship with doing wrong.

It may appear as if I have gotten off track. I haven't. I'm still talking about being unequally yoked. This discourse is still a part of my explanation of II Corinthians 6:14. Okay? Let's go one to the next phrase of that text: "…and what communion has light with darkness?"

The word "communion" is the Greek word *koinonia*, which means "social intercourse." So, ask yourself, what social intercourse does light have with darkness? The word intercourse means to come together in the same spirit, and for the same purpose. Can light come together with darkness? No! Light illuminates righteousness, and dissipates darkness. Darkness, on the other hand, covers unrighteousness, and hides evil. Such is the contrast between the believer and the unbeliever. That's why the believer shouldn't marry an unbeliever. There is no *communion* between the two.

Let me give you one more illustration concerning being unequally yoked, and I'll move on after this.

One of the best Biblical illustrations of being unequally yoked is the story of Samson and Delilah. Samson was a Hebrew, a worshiper of Almighty God, Jehovah. He was attracted to Delilah, a Philistine, who worshipped pagan gods. They had no spiritual commonality, whatsoever. His parents advised him to get a wife from his own nation, a woman who worshipped the same God. Samson wouldn't listen. He wanted to marry Delilah, because her physical beauty pleased him (Judges 14:3).

The Philistines were afraid of Samson's strength. They feared he would, one day, overpower them, and they would be enslaved.

They propositioned Delilah to help them discover from where he got his strength, so they could subdue him. Delilah agreed, and they paid her a large sum of money (Judges 16:5). After the Philistines captured Samson, they put his eyes out, and put him to work in the prison mill (Judges 16:21).

Samson never should have married Delilah. His demise came because he married the wrong woman, for the wrong reason. Delilah loved money more than she loved Samson. She was filled with greed, and he was filled with lust. Samson was dedicated for the work of God, but he forsook his calling, and went in accordance to his own desires. He married an unbeliever, and caused his own destruction, his own death.

I hope you have understood what I have said about marrying for love. I hope you see that the only way to get love is from God, and you must give your life to Him to receive it. He gives His spirit to you when you give your life to Him. That spirit is love. The joy comes when you find that other believer you want to spend the rest of your life with. Both of you will grow in love, and in the Spirit of God.

Don't think marriage is magical. It takes work. Good marriages are not created through osmosis. I mean, love is wonderful, but it has to be cultivated. It takes the work of both parties to make marriage a success. This is the type of work both spouses should enjoy when they really love each other. The joy of love is seeing the joy of the other person fulfilled. Too often, couples run to divorce court, when they have a problem they think they can't resolve.

Before you pay that retainer for an attorney, divorce is not an option for a believer. There are only two reasons a believer can divorce. One reason is this: When a believer is married to an unbeliever and the unbeliever leaves the marriage, the believer is not held accountable in that situation. Notice, I said if the unbeliever leaves. The believer can, then, remarry (I Corinthians 7: 13, 15). The other reason is because of adultery (Matthew 5: 32).

When both spouses are believers, neither spouse can leave the other, except for adultery. If one does decide to leave, neither spouse can remarry while the other spouse is still alive. We know this is not being observed, today. Many people remarry while the former spouse is still alive. According to Matthew 5:32, they are committing adultery with the new spouse.

Some people file for divorce after, convincing themselves, they don't love their spouses anymore. Now, we have already established, in an earlier chapter, that love is a spirit. This spirit of love, after He enters a believer, resides in the believer forever. How can someone fall out of love with another person? How can a person fall out of a divine spirit? They don't fall out of it, they reject it.

Previously, we discussed how love never fails, which is to say *that love does not fall away or drop off.* Love never stops loving. When a person says they don't love their spouse anymore, it was not love that left them, they left love. You cannot fall out of a spirit. You can, however, *reject* the spirit. When a person says they have fallen out of love with their spouse, there was no love there in the beginning, or they were "…Drawn away of his own lusts, and enticed." (James 1: 14)

I think that's enough talk about the spiritual legalities of divorce. I hope our little discussion has caused you to see how far all of us are from the way God intended things to be. Let us continue, now, and go a little further. Look at the following scripture. Let's talk a little about "sex and shacking."

> "Marriage is honourable in all, and the bed undefiled: but whoremongers and adulterers, God will judge." (Hebrews 13: 4)

It appears that marriage has become old fashioned, for a lot of people. It's not living together that's obsolete. It's the commitment people don't want. Now, cohabitation [shacking] is in. "Why buy the cow, when I can get the milk free?" Heard that, before? They live together, in a life of sin, just because sin is more convenient.

The above scripture says, "the marriage bed is undefiled." I know fornication is at an all-time high. Popularity doesn't make God accept it, though. Because everybody is doing something doesn't make God compromise His law. Sex is only sanctioned, by God, in marriage. Anything else is sin.

"Man, this is a new day. Things aren't like they were in the Bible days. This is a modern day. We are living in contemporary times, now. Why do I have to get married, to be with the one I want?" I know you've heard that before. You may have even said it yourself. I have. Well, let us see what the word of God has to say about that.

Hebrews 13:8 says, "Jesus Christ, the same yesterday, and today, and forever."

You think God changed his word, on sexual immorality, because times have become modern? No! Sex between two single people is still fornication. Likewise, if you are married, sex with a person who is not your spouse, is still adultery. Look at what Jesus said in Matthew 24:35. "Heaven and earth shall pass away, but my words shall not pass away." Whatever the word of God said, then, is still true, today. Truth doesn't change.

Since we've already talked about the first part of Hebrews 13:4, and have accepted that the marriage bed is undefiled, let's go on to the latter part of that scripture. It says, "...but God will judge whoremongers (fornicators) and adulterers."

God only approves of sex in marriage. He places all other sex in two categories---fornication and adultery. If two single people live together, and are having sexual relations, they are committing fornication. If a single person is living with a married person, and is having sexual relations, they are committing adultery. If a married or single person is living with a divorcee, and is having sexual relations, they are committing adultery. The Bible says they'll be judged by God. Do you get the feeling God hates shacking?

When it comes to judgment, the results can end with either condemnation or chastening. For the unsaved, Ephesians 5:5 says, "For this ye know, that no whoremonger (fornicator)... has any inheritance in the kingdom of Christ and of God." That means fornicators will be condemned to hell.

Now, there is a chance a fornicator can go to heaven. If he forsakes the life of fornication, and gives his life to Jesus Christ, all of his past sins will be forgiven. II Corinthians. 5:17 says, "Therefore, if any man be in Christ, he is a new creature: old things are passed away; behold, all things are become new." It is simple. Stop shacking and fornicating! Repent, and give your life to Jesus. Then, you'll be forgiven. You'll be transformed into a new person, and a new life, in the Lord, will be yours.

We have seen what happens to those who are unsaved, when they're judged. They are condemned to hell. Let's look, now, at what happens to the believer, when he's judged.

I Corinthians 11:32 says, "But when we are judged, we are chastened of the Lord, that we should not be condemned with the world."

If a believer is shacking, he is judged also. However, he's not condemned to hell. He's chastened by the Lord. Chastening is similar to a parent whipping his child, because he disobeyed him. Nowadays, whipping is considered child abuse. When children were spanked, when I was a child, we had good children. Today, children know they are not held accountable, and they do whatever they want, without any consequences. You tell me. What type of children do we have, now?

God is not subjected to the laws of man. He is the lawgiver, and he doesn't say that whipping your child is child abuse. As a matter of fact, God says, "He that spares the rod hates his son: but he that loves him chastens him betimes [early]" (Proverbs) 13:24).

In other words, the father who doesn't chastise his son, when he has been disobedient, doesn't care for his son. The failure to chastise your son will cause him to continue in that same behavior. So it is with God's reaction toward the believer, who lives in fornication. If God would turn His head from fornication, the believer would continue in it. It would, then, appear as if God hates his children, and approves of sin.

I know what a lot or you are saying. You think that because the Bible is an ancient book, it no longer has validity. That only shows you aren't relating the Bible to the times of today. You think God is behind the times. It was man who came up with the child abuse law, not God. That doesn't make God behind the times. That makes man behind the times. "For they being ignorant of God's righteousness, and going about to establish their own righteousness, haven't submitted themselves unto the righteousness of God."(Romans 10:3)

Let's finish this discussion on shacking, by looking at the last portion of Proverbs 13:24: "…but he that loves him chastens him betimes (early).

We've already stated that failing to chasten your son means you don't care for him. Chastening him, however, indicates you do care about where his life is headed. You don't wait until sin has become so familiar, it becomes a way of life. No! You chasten him early in life, before sin becomes a way of life, before it becomes a familiar mode of behavior.

So it is with God. He chastens the fornicator, because he loves him. He hates the sin, but He loves his child. He doesn't want that sin to become a way of life, so He chastens the fornicator early, to keep it from becoming a part of him. He teaches obedience through chastisement. As soon as repentance is made, the Lord begins chastisement, with the intention of restoration.

Sex has become so important; people want to know the sexual prowess of their intended, before they marry them. In other words, they want to test drive the car before they buy it. They don't want to marry someone, take a chance they are sexually incompatible, and they turn out not to be suited for each other. If God can pick the perfect mate for you, what makes you think He can't match you in that department, as well? God knows what He's doing. Trust Him! He knows what you like. He knows what you need.

Can we go a little further, and look at the roles of marriage? Let's see what the Word of God says about the duties of the wife, and the duties of the husband.

Wives Submit:

The word submit seems to create a certain level of reluctance in women. It doesn't mean that women are to be slaves for their husbands, without being able to speak what's on their minds. If that were so, husbands would be nothing more than pimps, or slave masters. They would have total control over their wives, and the wives would be allowed to do nothing, but whatever the husband said. As always, the Word of God has the answer we need. It's from the Word that we get truth. Look at what he scripture says.

> "Wives submit yourselves to your own husbands, as unto the Lord. For the husband is the head of the wife, even as Christ is the head of the church: and he is the head of the body. Therefore as the church is subject unto Christ, so let the wives be to their husbands in everything." (Ephesians 5:22-24)

First of all, the above scripture says that "wives should submit to their own husbands, as if they are submitting to the Lord." Do not panic! The word Lord simply means *one who has authority.* This merely means that wives are to recognize the authority God has given the husband. *He is the head of his wife, just as Christ is the head of the church.* We really have to stop here, and offer an interpretation. This needs to be totally understood, if the wife is going to *joyfully* submit to her husband. You aren't to submit to someone else's husband. You must, however, submit to your own.

The above scripture says the husband is the head of his wife, as Christ is the head of the church. Let's look at the headship of Christ, over the church. What qualifies Christ to be the head of the church? The same qualities will have to undoubtedly be in the husband. Let us compare.

1. Christ sacrificed for the church.	1. Husbands must sacrifice for their wives
2. Christ teaches the church	2. Husbands must teach their wives
3. Christ leads the church	3. Husbands must lead their wives
4. Crist empowers the church	4. Husbands must empower their wives
5. Christ protects the church	5. Husbands must protect their wives
6. Christ provides for the church	6. Husbands must provide for their wives
7. Christ prays for the church	7. Husbands must pray for their wives
8. Christ forgives the church	8. Husbands must forgive their wives
9. Christ loves unconditionally	9. Husbands must love unconditionally
10. Christ gives the church mercy	10. Husbands must also extend mercy

Without a doubt, the husband has authority. Should the wife submit to the office of authority, or to the practice of authority? Let me explain what I mean. A person can have the position of authority, but in name only. In other words, he has the position, but he doesn't do what the position entails. He's just occupying space. As a result of his negligence, no one respects him as the person in charge. Even though he has the position of authority, no one follows him, or obeys him. His authority is in name only.

If husbands want their wives to submit to them, they have to be as Christ is to the church—a servant. Authority does not mean "giving orders," and not doing anything else. To whom much is given, much is required. Authority means "giving yourself." If husbands adhere to the above-mentioned ten points, wives would *joyfully* submit to their husbands. Men, stop bossing, and start serving.

Some women think they can leave their husbands, or stop their submission to him, if he fails to fulfill his position of authority. No! That is not true. Unless the husband has committed adultery, the wife has no grounds for divorce. She should stay with her husband, continue to live the Christian life before him, and pray that God would restore him to fulfilling his position of authority.

There is a myth regarding the submission of the wife. Let us clear this up right now. Some people think if the wife makes more money than the husband, she doesn't have to submit to him. Many women think the more financially independent they are, the less they need their husbands. They think that, because they don't need his help to pay the bills, they don't need him, at all. Of course, that's not true. There are two scriptures that come to mind, concerning this issue. Let's look at them, now. The first one reads as follows:

"...Take heed, and beware of covetousness: for a man's life consisteth not in the abundance of the things which he possesseth." (Luke 12:15)

This scripture begins with a warning. God cautions us to guard ourselves against greed and idolatry. Covetousness is greed, and in some cases, idle worship. It can be fraudulent and extortionary. Greed comes when someone desires what another person has, and in reality, they don't need it. It can be material possessions, or it can be position.

There's nothing wrong with a wife making money, even when it supersedes her husband. If she craves, however, more money to be free of her husband, or to usurp his authority, her desires, then, are covetous, filled with greed and idolatry. It's greed, when she craves what she doesn't need, and wants to possess what's not entitled to her. It's idolatry, because she craves an authoritative position that belongs to her husband. That craving is the same as worshipping. When an idea enters your mind, it causes you to dream about it, long for it, meditate on it, as if it were some type of god. You submit to it, because you want it to be a part of your life. You start to adore the idea, and believe you really deserve to have it.

Wealth and riches don't make you who you are. Regardless of the wealth of a married woman, she is still a wife. She isn't independent of her husband because she happens to be rich. Neither does she have authority over her husband because she's rich. Her riches should be assets for her household, not a means to belittle her husband. God will never bless role reversal.

I told you I had two scriptures I wanted to mention. We've already talked about the first one. The second one reads as follows:

"But I would have you know, that the head of every man is Christ; and the head of the

woman is the man; and the head of Christ is
God." (1 Corinthians 11:3)

While some women may want to create their own hierarchy,
God has already established one. The scripture above says, "…
the head of every man is Christ." That means that man follows
the guidelines of Christ. He is led by his Word, and the Holy
Spirit. His life glorifies Jesus. Man is the glory of God. When
you see him, you don't actually see him. You see the Christ that
lives within him.

The "B" portion of the text says, "…and the head of the
woman is the man." As the husband follows Christ, he conveys
the same guidelines that are governing his life, to his wife. In that
process, the man glorifies Christ, his head. The woman glorifies
her husband, who is her head. And they all glorify God.

The husband glorifies Christ by following his ways. The
woman glorifies her husband by following him, as he follows
Christ. It's not a woman's wealth that glorifies her husband. It's
the righteousness of Christ, handed down to her, through her
husband. Because of that, people don't see them, when they look
upon them. They see the Christ that lives within them.

A woman can't be in the position of man. She'll never have
that authority. That's not the way God designed it. Both have roles
to fulfill. Making more money than a man doesn't make a woman
a man. Neither does it change her role designed by God. Rich or
not, the head of the wife is still her husband. She is to be subject
to him in everything, just as the church is subject to Christ.

We need to look at how the church is subject to Christ.
This will help women know how they should be subject to their
husbands

The church is comprised of the *igglesia*. The Greek meaning
of that word is *"the called out ones."* The church is not the building
people meet in every Sunday. The church is the people who meet

there. They're the *called out ones*. They've been called out of darkness into the marvelous light. They've been called out of the world and renewed, by the transformation of their minds. These *called out believers* are subject unto Christ in all things. Let's look at how, because the wife is subject unto her husband the same way.

First of all, the church submits to Christ readily. Although that submission is readily, it is also voluntarily. The church is not forced to submit to Christ. She does so because she wants to. Why does she want to? She trusts Christ! He has already proven his love, by dying on the cross for her. He didn't wait for the church to love him. He loved her first.

Christ loved the church, in spite of her short-comings. He accepted the bad with the good. He didn't judge her. Instead, he washed her with his word. He transformed her, so she would look like him, and glorify him. Those are just a few of the reasons why the church submits to Christ. These same reasons should be why wives submit to their husbands. Look at the list of ten things previously mentioned. Even that list doesn't exhaust every reason why the church submits to Christ.

Let me caution you women, before I go on. In your submission to the man of your choice [women are the choosers, while men are the hunters], some men are good at pretending that Christ is the head of their lives.

As I have mentioned before, we live in the era of the pimp and player. They emulate this scripture, to keep their women under control. Instinctively, most women already know they must have a man to lead and teach them. Where they go wrong is, the men they choose don't have Christ as the head of their lives. They are not filled with the Holy Spirit, and they are not guided by the Word of God. Instead, they are led by a body of knowledge called *game*. God is not glorified in *game*.

As women learn this knowledge called *game*, they become skilled in deception, lying, betrayal, manipulation, and sexual immorality. They are exploited, and used by those who teach them. They become enslaved, and are placed in bondage. Not only do they do the things the new knowledge dictates, they become comfortable with their new titles. Those titles don't glorify God. Women, be careful to whom you submit.

We aren't going to just talk about the submission of the wife, and don't say anything about the husband. Let's look at what the Word says about what the husband is commanded to do in marriage.

Husbands Love Your Wives:

We have already discovered the role of the wife. Her job is to submit to her husband, as he leads her. The question is: How does the husband lead his wife? As usual, the Word of God has the answer. Let's look at the word and discover what God has to say concerning this issue.

> "Husbands, love your wives, even as Christ also loved the church, and gave himself for it; That he may sanctify and cleanse it with the washing of water by the word, That he might present it to himself a glorious church, not having spot, or wrinkle, or any such thing; but that it should be holy and without blemish. So ought men to love their wives as their own bodies. He that loves his wife loves himself. For no man ever yet hated his own flesh; but nourishes and cherishes it, even as the Lord the church." (Ephesians 5: 25-29)

When I read this text, the first thing that comes to mind is sacrifice. Christ sacrificed himself for his bride, the church. How?

He gave himself for it, by dying on the cross. Why? He wanted to purify and consecrate her by washing her with the Word, to present her to himself, in a holy and purified state.

It's not money, or a great career, that makes a wife as great as she can be. It's the Word of God, which is fed to her by her husband. The inclination to sin is washed away. Bad habits and bad behaviors are washed away. Rude and insulting conversation is changed into words that edify. The old person is buried, and a new person, in Christ, is arisen.

Just as Christ sacrificed for the church, so should the husband sacrifice for his wife. She should come first, and he should place himself last. Sacrifice is not always monetary. There are more sacrifices he can make. It depends on the need, and the situation.

Remember! There's no real sacrifice unless something is relinquished that you really treasured, or wanted. If a person calls himself making a sacrifice of something, and after the sacrifice, there remain two or three of the same things supposedly sacrificed, that's not sacrifice.

Suppose you see a homeless person hungry, and you want to help him? All you have in your possession are ten dollars. You give him five of the ten, and you keep the other five. You did help the homeless person. Don't call it a sacrifice, though. It was not a sacrifice, because you didn't give the whole ten dollars. You kept five for yourself. You did think about his need, but you also thought about your own. That's not sacrifice. When real sacrifice is made, you feel the pinch.

We say God sacrificed his Son for us, because he gave his *only* Son. He didn't have but one, but he gave all he had. That's sacrifice. When a husband sacrifices for his wife, he has to consider the magnitude of her need. To sacrifice means to give all you can to meet that need, even if it's something you wanted for yourself.

Okay! Let us go a little further, in our discussion. The above-mentioned text doesn't just say the husband should sacrifice for his wife. It also gives the reason for the sacrifice—that he may *sanctify* and *cleanse* her by the washing of the Word. What does sanctify and cleanse actually mean?

It must be understood, at this point, the husband is the priest of his household. It's his duty to teach the word of God, and to evangelize every member of his family for the Lord. He begins by *consecrating* and *purifying* his wife, with the Word of God. In doing so, he *sanctifies* his wife. It's the husband's duty to help his wife be Christ-like. If Christ is his head, Christ will be passed to the wife, and everyone will glorify God. Let's see, now, what components are in the word of God that enables a husband to sanctify his wife.

> "All scripture is given by inspiration of God, and is profitable for doctrine (instruction), for reproof (conviction), for correction (reformation), for instruction in righteousness (character, quality of being right or just): that the man of God may be perfect (mature, complete), throughly furnished unto all good works (fitted out)." (II Timothy 3:16, 17)

When a wife is sanctified, she is *"set apart."* She is no longer ordinary. She is unique, different, and peculiar. She is nothing like the women of the world. She exudes the presence of God, the character of God, and the love of God. She stands out, and her presence is noticeable to all.

She doesn't have to say anything, her being is evident she has been with Jesus. Those who know God, love her. Those who don't know God, are jealous of her. Of course, she doesn't become the wife of every man's dream on her own. No! This sanctification takes place through the Word of God. Let's look at how the word of God does that.

The first thing the above-mentioned text says is the Word of God is profitable for doctrine, which is *instruction*. Some women hate to be instructed. They hate to be told what to do. If she wants to glorify God, though, she has to learn what God expects of her. She must learn to do things the way God wants them done. After all, it's not her will, but the will of God that must be done.

Another way the word works in sanctification is through "reproof." God is *omniscient.* He has all knowledge, and he knows our short-comings. His word reproves us, which means his word *convicts* us of our faults. This conviction isn't to belittle us, embarrass us, or to humiliate us. The purpose of this type of conviction is to show us what we need to change, in order to be more like him. It's like looking in a mirror. Sometimes, the view is ugly. Sometimes, the view brings shame. Nevertheless, change must take place.

That's when the Word of God helps us in *correction*. Once we discover our imperfections, we have no power to make the necessary changes. Reformation can only come through the Word of God. As one learns and obeys the Word, a new person is created gradually. She is transformed into what God intended her to be, into the wife God intended her to be. Old habits are erased, and old concepts about what a wife should be are changed. Be aware, though. This is a life-long process. This doesn't take place overnight. Sanctification is not an immediate metamorphosis. You never reach perfection. You do, however, continue to strive for it.

Another occurrence that takes place in sanctification is *instruction in righteousness.* This means two things. Your character is shaped into the image of Christ, and you start doing things the way God wants them done. You no longer do things based on feelings, emotions, or impulsiveness. The Word of God creates in you a new behavior. It becomes your guide, and your standard for all things. You truly, then, become the righteousness of God.

We've seen how a person is changed by the Word of God, in the process of sanctification. Now, let's see why God requires such a process. The last portion of the above-mentioned text [II Timothy 3: 17] says, "…that the man of God may be perfect; throughly furnished unto all good works."

The process of sanctification matures us, and qualifies us to do good works. You may ask, why must a person be qualified to do good things? Aren't we already qualified? No! What we think is good, is not good. Isaiah 64: 6 says, "But we are all as an unclean thing, and all our righteousnesses are as filthy rags…" God looks at, what we call good works, as filthy rags.

The word rags refer to the bandages soldiers used in war, to cover their wounds. They were filled with blood, nasty tissue, and puss. In the Bible days, there was no gauze or band aids. These rags went next to the wound. Nothing separated the rags from the blood and other contaminations. Just like the Word of God says, they were filthy. Human righteousness is just like those rags. Therefore, not only does God qualify a wife to do good works, He also equips her to do them. She doesn't implement her own righteousness. She becomes the righteousness of God in sanctification.

I think that's enough about sanctification. We've discussed what it is, why it has to happen, and the power the Word of God has to make it happen. We are still discussing Ephesians 5: 25-29. Let us finish this text by indulging ourselves into verses 28 and 29. They read as follows:

> "So ought men to love their wives as their own bodies. He that loves his wife loves himself. For no man yet ever hated his own flesh; but nourishes and cherishes it, even as the Lord the church…"
> (Ephesians 5:28-29)

If you see a man abusing his wife, he doesn't love himself. The man, who loves his wife, loves himself. The Bible says a man should love his wife like he loves his own body. No one hates his own body. He doesn't abuse and hurt his body. Instead, he nourishes and cherishes it. Do you see Christ abusing his body, the church? No! He nourishes and cherishes it. Husbands should love their wives in like manner.

Let's look at these two words---nourish and cherish--- and see what they mean. Undoubtedly, the meaning of these two words will give us more insight, into how a husband should love his wife.

Nourish means to *"bring up, to train, or to help mature."* That's what a man does to his own body. He doesn't let his body go down. He trains it, in the gym, to make it strong and beautiful. He wants a body others like looking at. He doesn't want it to look like and old man, with a gut, at the age of twenty-five. No! He wants it to mature chronologically, and grow at the pace it should. He wants it to be healthy, with strength and endurance. In the same way, husbands should nourish their wives.

The Greek meaning of *cherish* is to "heat, or to soften by heat." The word heat makes one think of warmth, like a bird warming her young, with her feathers. This type of warmth brings comfort. Husbands should extend this type of tender loving care to comfort their wives. It makes them feel valued. It makes them feel important. They'll know they are loved, even if the rest of the world doesn't love them. Their self-esteem won't be diminished. Instead, it will be uplifted.

Comfort erases fear. It creates the assurance of safety and protection. When safety and protection are present, worry is absent. There's very little anxiety, when a person feels safe and protected. Instead of a feeling of anxiety, there's a feeling of security. A wife must feel secure in the love of her husband. She must feel safe and protected. That's how Christ loves the church. Husbands should love their wives the same way.

CHAPTER 8

LOVE AND THE CHURCH

If there were a place you should find love, it ought to be in the church. Why? Because God is love, and every member of the household of faith, has God's spirit in them. Therefore, love should be present. You should see it in action. You should feel it at the door, when you are greeted. Love ought to be in the air, in the atmosphere. When Sunday morning comes around, people ought to rush to the church, because they can hardly wait to get there. After a week at the job, dealing with people of the world who don't know Christ, church should be an environment of comfort and joy.

The love of God is unconditional. It is nonjudgmental. When you go to church, no one should judge you based on how you look, how you dress, how you smell, what you drive, where you work, if you work, where you live, or by how much money you make. You don't have to be prequalified by anyone the to be in the presence of God.

Don't go to church looking for perfection. The church is not perfect. And when I talk about the church, I'm not talking about the building people worship in. Those who have accepted Christ as Lord and Saviour are the church. They are the *igglesia*—the called out ones. Everyone who has accepted Christ has been called out of something. Some were called out of drugs, prostitution, homosexuality, crime, sexual immorality, murder, so-on and so-on.

Many will say they haven't done any of those things. That may be true. They may have not committed any of those sins. Those visible sins, however, aren't the only sins. What about pride, greed, idolatry, self-righteousness, covetousness, envy, and jealousy? These are sins that are invisible, but they are sins, just the same. The church has been called out from all of those. Remember! Jesus came to save those who are lost, not those who are perfect.

Please, don't make the mistake of thinking that everyone that gathers on Sunday morning is the church. Everyone there on Sunday isn't filled with the Holy Spirit, which means everyone doesn't have the spirit of love. Those who don't have the Spirit aren't saved. Therefore, they aren't members of the church. Neither are they members of God's family.

Having your name on the church role doesn't make you a member of the church. Being baptized doesn't even make you a member of the church. You must accept Jesus as Lord and Savior and, thereafter, be filled with the Holy Spirit. Then, you are filled with the presence of God, as well as the love of God. You, then, become one of the "called out ones," and are a member of God's family.

The church is the body of Christ, as well as the bride of Christ. She should embody the character of Christ. She should forgive like Christ, have mercy like Christ, and love like Christ. She should have the power of Christ, the knowledge of Christ, and the peace of Christ. The church ought to look like Christ. No church is perfect, in this area, however. This is a process that takes time.

When looking for a church to join, you must be very discerning. You can't join any church. Some people join church because their friend is a member. Some join church to find a wife, or a husband. Some join church because the choir sings well, and the band plays the type of music they like. Some people also join church because it doesn't hold services too long, and is very close to their homes. Of course, those aren't good reasons to join church.

A good church is one that preaches and teaches the Word of God from the Authorized King James Version. That's my preference. Not from one of the modern translations that have changed the meaning of the original word. Desire the purity of God's word, not man's interpretation that changes the word, to give it his meaning.

Jesus went about doing good. He fed the hungry, healed the sick, freed the captives, preached the good news to the poor, mended the broken-hearted, gave sight to the blind, and raised the dead back to life.

The church ought to have ministries that also meet the needs of the poor, the broken-hearted, the blind (those walking in darkness), and raise the spiritually dead back to life. How many times have you seen churches that reside in impoverished environments, do nothing to change the community? The church continues to grow and prosper, but the community continues to diminish. That's not a good display of the love of Jesus Christ.

Church isn't what she used to be. There are so many churches that have a form of godliness, but they deny the power thereof. On the outside, they look like a church. However, on the inside, God is not present. You have to be careful. That superficial display can deceive you, and lure you in. It's a trick of the enemy, Satan. You do realize he goes to church, too, don't you?

It appears Satan has infiltrated the church, and has placed his ministers in the pulpit. I have visited churches, and found many of them to be nothing more than covens for the enemy. I looked for the people of God, and found none. There was no display of the spirit of God. A contrary spirit was there. Love wasn't present. And this is what I believe happened.

In church, after the sermon is preached, it is customary to extend an invitation. This is what I've seen. When people come up to the front, at invitation time, there's usually a cadre of people to receive them. These people are there to explain what has spiritually happened to them, in order to help them understand this first phase of salvation.

When the people went to the front, the waiting cadre of people immediately laid hands on them. I recalled when I was saved. I went down the middle isle, and I was crying like a baby. No one laid hands on me. I asked myself. Has God created a new way for us to give our lives to him? I searched for that in the Bible. I never found where it said the laying on of hands was a prerequisite of salvation.

When I asked one of the ministers who stood up front at invitation time, what that was all about, he said they did that to impart the Holy Spirit into the new believer. I asked, "Why? Did God need help, now, giving His spirit to whom He wanted to have it?" I mean, really! I thought that was how the new believer came to Christ, in the first place, by the power of the Holy Spirit (John 6:44).

The worst thing a person can do is assume the person laying hands on him has the Holy Spirit. The laying on of hands is how spirits are transferred from one person to another. If you don't know the person laying hands on you, how do you know the spirit transferred into you isn't a demonic spirit? The only way to be sure is not to let anyone lay hands on you, especially if you don't know them. Be careful. This is how the devil infiltrates the church, and makes disciples.

In most of the churches I've visited, that's the way they do things. People are being deceived. They think they are getting the

Holy Spirit when, in reality, they are receiving a demonic spirit. They begin to worship that spirit, praise that spirit, follow that spirit, and obey that spirit. All the time, they think God is who they are obeying. Before you know it, the entire church is filled with people with that spirit. In a church such as that, there's no love.

When a church places more emphasis on the spirit than on Jesus, that church isn't teaching the Word of God. They believe in another spirit, other than the Holy Spirit. I say that because the Word of God says the Holy Spirit glorifies Jesus (John 16: 13-15). Therefore, it's impossible for the spirit in a church to be of God, and not glorify Jesus. That's the job of the Holy Spirit. The Holy Spirit manifests Jesus Christ.

The church is made up of people who should be, not just hearers of the word, but doers of the word also. Like I said before, the church isn't perfect. There are various categories of people in the church. Every little group has its own identity (Luke 8: 5-15). Everyone doesn't hear the word. Here are some of the various groups you will encounter.

The Unattentive:

There are people who come to church, and they receive no benefits therefrom, because they don't pay attention to the Word of God. They hear the Word, but it doesn't register. They are too busy tweeting, texting, or emailing someone. It just falls by the wayside. Because the Word isn't absorbed, the devil comes and steals the word from them.

The Hardhearted:

Some people hear the word, but they fail to cultivate what goes into their hearts. Like any seed, the Word of God has to be watered. A hard heart is dry, and has no water. It's like a rock. Any seed planted in a hard heart will not grow, or survive. When seeds are sown into a hard heart, they come up and wither from the lack of moisture.

The Distracted:

When the seed of the word is planted among thorns, both of them grow together, and the thorns end up choking the Word. The thorns represent the cares and pleasures of this world. When they distract the believer, they choke the word of God. Distractions of this world prevent the Word of God from ripening and bearing fruit.

The Fruit Bearers:

Sometimes, the Word of God falls on good ground, and bears fruit. Good ground is the heart of people who hear the Word, retain it, and obey it. They continue along those lines until they bear fruit. Their fruit blesses others, and glorifies God. These are the disciples of Christ. They are the ones through whom love is identified in the church. Let us examine this concept a little closer, and see what the Word of God says about it.

The Evidence Of Love In The Church:

"By this shall all men know that you are my disciples, if ye have love one to another." (John 1:35)

The only way love is seen in the church, is through the disciples of Jesus Christ. The word disciple means "one who learns in order to do." They're the ones who learn the teachings of Jesus, in order to incorporate them into their lives. There's one commandment that teaches them to "love your neighbor as yourself" (Matthew. 22:39). This commandment, when obeyed, validates them as disciples of Jesus Christ. When others see this love, they know God is present.

When there's bickering and fighting, it's not of God. James 3:16 says, "Where envying and strife is, there is confusion and every evil work." The church shouldn't be a place of confusion and evil. Why? "Because God is not the author of confusion, but of peace, as in all churches of the saints" (I Corinthians. 14:35). If you see evil and confusion in the church, God didn't cause it. The devil did. God is a God of love. And when "the called out ones" love one another the presence of God can be seen by others.

Where are the true disciples of Christ? Where is the love in the church? I have visited churches, and no one spoke to me. Yeah! Everyone greets you after you're asked to stand, because it's your first time there. But does love have to be ordered? Do you have to tell people to show love to another person? Those greetings are only part of a ritual. They don't come from the heart. What ever happened to that love that makes you feel like someone really cares?

Shall we, now, look at what the church looks like, when love is in the church? Not the pretense of love, acting as if you love someone, when you really don't. Neither am I talking about love given through one of the rituals of the church. No! I'm not talking about love given through habit, duty, or routine. I'm talking about the actual love of God. Let's take a look.

Freedom To Praise And Worship:

II Corinthians. 3:17 says, "Where the spirit of the Lord is, there is liberty." When the spirit of the Lord is present in the church, not only is there liberty (freedom), there is also love. People should be free to praise and worship God, as the spirit leads them.

Have you ever been in a church that was so quiet, when you said hallelujah, everyone looked at you, as if to say, shut up. You couldn't shout, or clap your hands in praise. All you could do was sit in silence, because shouting and praising God aloud was against regular decorum.

What type of church would prohibit worship, and harness the praise of God, for the sake of image and sophistication? Look at what the Word of God says about praising God.

> "Enter into his gates with thanksgiving, and into his courts with praise: be thankful unto him, and bless his name." (Psalms 100:4)

When love is in the church, there will also be praise and worship. Praise will be there to thank God for the things he has done, because there's thanksgiving in praise. When you love someone, you appreciate him. You thank him, to show your appreciation. We ought to come into the church with praise on our lips. That's why David says, in Psalms 34:1, "I will bless the Lord at all times: His praise shall continually be in my mouth." He appreciated what God had done for him, and he showed God his appreciation by praising Him.

Worship is different. Worship isn't given because of what God has done for you. Instead, worship is given to God because of who He is. Submission and adoration are given to God to honor is character, and his attributes. God's greatness ought to be expressed in the church. His attributes should be worshipped. If there is love for God, worship will also be present.

Those who attempt to stop you from worshipping God, for the sake of image and sophistication, have no love for God. They are legalists. Legalists follow a group of rules. They follow a routine, and they worship out of duty, not from the heart. When someone places the church constitution above God, he is a legalist. If they place traditions above the Word of God, they are legalists. When the rules of the church are more important than following the spirit of God, love isn't present in that church.

Freedom To Serve:

When there's love in the church, there's also freedom to serve him. So many churches, today, require you be qualified to serve God. Some choirs even hold auditions, in order to obtain, what they call qualified singers. Many churches even require pastors to have a certain level of education, before they can apply for the position. And so many pastors have the credentials, but they don't have the spirit (power) of God. As a result, many churches are dead. God isn't there! They wanted education, instead of the power of God. Look at what Paul says, in the word of God, about that.

> "And I, brethren, when I came to you, came not with excellency of speech or of wisdom, declaring unto you the testimony of God. For I determined not to know anything among you, save Christ, and him crucified... And my speech and my preaching was not with enticing words of man's wisdom, but in demonstration of the Spirit and of power: That your faith should stand not in

the wisdom of men, but in the power of God."
(I Corinthians. 2: 1-2, 4-5)

Paul is saying, in the scripture above, his resume may not include degrees from the halls of academia. "I do, however, come demonstrating the spirit and the power of God. I do not have any enticing words to give you, because I do not claim to know anything, except the gospel of Christ, and him crucified. I may not have matriculated in the finest schools, but one thing I do know. I know him who was once dead, but now lives forever more."

Paul goes on to say, "I do this in order for you put your faith in the right thing. I don't exalt myself, because I don't want you to place your faith in man. No! I want you to put your faith in God. All power belongs to God. Therefore, I demonstrate his power for you to trust in him, and in him alone."

My question is: How can a church qualify someone to serve God, when they don't how to. It's God who qualifies people. His standards aren't like ours. His thoughts aren't like our thoughts. We look at the outside appearance, but God looks inside. The efforts of the church to qualify people for service don't enhance service, it restricts it.

I had a friend, who was also a preacher. In his early years of ministry, after he graduated from seminary, my friend felt his calling was to be a pastor. Unfortunately, the pastor he was under tried to qualify him, or should I say disqualify him. Whenever my friend heard of a church that was looking for a pastor, he would send his resume, and tell his pastor he was trying for the position. He felt keeping his pastor informed was the right thing to do. After all, his pastor would have to give him references.

My friend's pastor never gave him the green light to pursue his dream. He would always say, "I think you should wait. You don't have enough experience for a church like that." My friend finally realized his pastor was trying to hold him back. Maybe it was jealousy. The real reason never became apparent. My friend finally left that church, and is now pastoring a church of his own. It's tragic that preachers try to stop other preaches from serving God.

A lot of people would be shocked to know this, and even may not believe it. There are preachers who backlist or blackball other preachers, to stop them from preaching anywhere in a particular city. When did man get the authority to decide who may, or may not serve God? What? You thought the Pharisees were dead? Well, they are still living. They are in every denomination, still trying to control the religious world, by keeping Jesus out. Of course, they try to remain secretive, but they still exist. Anyone serving, in one of their churches, must comply by their rules, not the Bible.

When love is in the church, there are other things that should exist. Let's look at the following:

Love For The Unfortunate And Displaced:

If the church is to show love, she must show it for those who are unfortunate and displaced. The church can no longer be more concerned for her image, than she is for the hurting and downtrodden. She has to be a refuge for those who have no one to care for them, for those who are abused, molested, and heartbroken. If anyone had love for the unfortunate, it was Jesus. He wasn't a capitalist, like the Pharisees. He had a genuine concern for the people. Listen to what he says in the Word of God.

> "The spirit of the Lord is upon me, because he
> hath anointed me to preach the gospel to the poor;
> he hath sent me to heal the brokenhearted, to

preach deliverance to the captives, and recovering
of sight to the blind, to set at liberty them that
are bruised, to preach the acceptable year of the
Lord." (Luke 4: 18-19)

According to the scripture above, Jesus was anointed
(empowered) by God to help the unfortunate. He didn'ot come
to help the rich, or the privileged. He came to help the displaced,
and the rejected. Let's go down the list of people in the scripture
above, and talk a little bit about each one.

The first group of people mentioned is the *poor*. Jesus said he
came to preach "good news" to the poor. Good news is the Greek
meaning of the word gospel. When the gospel is preached in the
church, it should be good news. The poor should hear good news.
They should hear that they don't have to be poor, and live the way
they are living. Someone needs to tell them that Jesus came that
they might have life, and have it more abundantly (John 10:10).

The poor suffers from not having enough to make ends meet.
They are the people who go on welfare. They are those who are on
food stamps. They are the unemployed, who have trouble paying
rent every month. The poor are the homeless, who often commit
crimes, in order to eat. They are the people who resort to alcohol
and drugs, because they have lost hope of ever living a better
life. The poor can't afford the latest fashion. They're laughed at,
when they come to church. They're the ones who need to hear
the good news.

The church is filled with people who came from the same
backgrounds. They went without, and were hungry, and couldn't
make ends meet. They, too, lived in poverty. Some of them grew
up in the projects. They didn't have a car. They rode public
transportation every day. Some even wore hand-me-down clothes,
because their parents couldn't afford new ones.

It appears that some people in the church have forgotten where they came from. Now, they think they are better than the poor people that come to their churches. They have forgotten that it was God who brought them out of the ghetto. It was God who gave them better jobs, and better incomes. Their lives haven't improved because they deserved it. No! It was because of God's grace, and nothing else. God blessed them with what they didn't deserve. Instead of laughing at the poor, they should tell them what God has done for them, he can do for them, too. That's the good news!

The next group of people the above-mentioned scripture points out is the *brokenhearted*. Those are people who have been crushed. Their emotions and mind have been shattered. Perhaps their dreams were shattered. Maybe they were rejected. The Bible doesn't give a reason for the broken-heartedness. It could be a number of things. Whatever the reason, the brokenhearted needs to be healed.

So many people come to church whose lives are drenched with failure, with thoughts of suicide. Either they want to kill themselves, or they want to kill someone else. Some think their lives are over, because their dreams haven't come true. Many are shattered because they loved someone who didn't love them. Rejection made them feel worthless, useless, without any value. They come to the church to be healed.

Who knows more about the brokenhearted than Jesus? "He was despised and rejected of men; a man of sorrows, and acquainted with grief" (Isaiah 53:3). We, the disciples of Jesus, can help restore hope back into the lives of the brokenhearted, by giving them Jesus. Most of us have testimonies about how Jesus healed us. We need to tell what the Lord has done for us. Let the brokenhearted know they are not alone. Extend to them the love of Jesus, and they shall be healed.

What else does the above mentioned scripture say Jesus came to do? He came "to preach deliverance to the captives". When we think about a captive, we think of someone enslaved, confined, or held hostage. The church has to consider these people, because there are so many of them. We all are enslaved to something, and we all need deliverance.

We are already aware of the enslavement of drugs, alcohol, gambling, and sex. No doubt, people are being held hostage by those things. What about the other things that hold us hostage? Things like pride, self-righteousness, covetousness, greed, envy, and jealousy, should be considered also. People are enslaved by those things, as well.

Some people come to church to be delivered. No one wants to be enslaved. No one wants to be confined to a bad habit. No one wants to be held hostage. People want to be free. They just don't know how to obtain that freedom.

When a person is held captive, they are a prisoner of the devil. He has erected, in the minds of so many, strongholds. Even some of God's children fit this category. To be delivered from a stronghold is a battle. Every captive is in the fight of his life, because the devil wants to kill and destroy him. The church has the necessary weapons to help the captive. She must arm captives with those weapons, and train them to fight the enemy. Look at what the word of God says about this matter.

> "For the weapons of our warfare are not carnal, but mighty through God to the pulling down of strongholds; Casting down imaginations, and every high thing that exalts itself against the knowledge of God, and bringing into captivity every thought to the obedience of Christ..." (II Corinthians 10: 4-5)

The battle is in the mind. He devil sets up strongholds in the mind. That's his method of enslaving people. But the church has weapons of warfare that are mighty through God, to pull down the devil's strongholds. These weapons are able to cast down every imagination, and every high thought, that exalts itself against the knowledge of God. They will bring into captivity every thought into the obedience of Christ. You are probably asking, what are these weapons?

The best weapon is the Word of God. It has the capacity to transform a person, by renewing his mind. It causes a person to become a new person, and develop a new way of thinking (II Corinthians. 5:17), tearing down the devil's stronghold, in the process.

Another good weapon is praise. Praise puts God first, and makes a person recognize his sovereignty. Praise is filled with thanksgiving. It lets you know where your blessings come from. Praise enlightens you to the fact that, without God, you could do nothing. You begin to notice that he is your strength, and "his strength is made perfect in your weakness." (II Corinthians. 12:9).

Prayer is also a very good weapon for spiritual warfare. It gets you in touch with God. You can approach the one, who fights your battles, and worship him, as well as converse with him. In prayer, you can ask for direction. You can express your desires and needs. God is able to inform you about what to do concerning various problems.

One thing about prayer is you can't wait until disaster occurs, before you begin to pray. You must have a consistent prayer life. You have to talk to God on a daily basis. It will do you no good to start talking to God, when the devil attacks you. That would be a little too late. What are you going to draw out of your heavenly account, when you haven't made a deposit in a year? Sorry! Your account is empty. Pray without ceasing.

God is not a remote control God. He doesn't jump whenever you push a button. God is a relationship God. You must spend some time with him in prayer. Get to know him. Build a relationship with him. Then, when you call, he'll answer. Remember Daniel? (Daniel 6)

Daniel was a man who consistently prayed. He didn't wait until trouble appeared, to start praying. He prayed three times a day. The king passed a law that no one could pray to any other god, except to him, for thirty days, under the penalty of being thrown into the lion's den.

Daniel didn't stop praying. He kept his normal routine of praying three times a day. When he was found out, and thrown into the lion's den, God came to his rescue. He closed the mouths of the lions, and they didn't do Daniel any harm. He didn't wait until the devil attacked him, before he started praying. He was consistent in prayer, and God answered him.

If the church would teach these weapons of warfare to those who fight for the captives, they would be delivered.

Another thing Jesus did was to "help recover the sight of the blind." We know Jesus literally restored sight to the blind. However, I believe this reference of the blind is also metaphorical. The Greek meaning of the word blind, in this text, refers *to being wrapped in smoke, conceited, or to have one's head in the clouds.* In other words, it means to be filled with pride.

Jesus came to the house of Israel. Israel, on the other hand, had gotten besides herself. She started to believe she was more than she actually was. She had gotten bigheaded, and was blinded by her own pride. Jesus wanted to restore her sight. He wanted to help her come out of darkness into the light. She didn't think she was in darkness. She thought Jesus was in darkness, and rejected him.

Many people live in darkness. They come to the church looking for direction. He who walks in darkness can't find his way.

He can't see where he's going, and stumbles along the pathway of life. The church has to be that beacon of light. She has to help the blind recover their sight, by bringing them out of darkness into the marvelous light. That light is Jesus Christ.

Jesus also came to "set at liberty them that are bruised," which means he came *to free them that were oppressed.* Jesus was born into a world of oppression. The Pharisees oppressed the people by using legalism to rule the religious world. The Romans oppressed the people with government, taxes, and the military. They were being bruised from both ends. Jesus came to liberate them.

A person is oppressed when his will is being controlled by someone else. He is unable to do what he wants, or what he thinks is right. He has to do what someone else wants, or he suffers punishment. How many people do you know that are under that type of oppression? Is it a boss, a spouse, a fraternity of friends that oppresses them? Whatever the case may be, someone needs to tell them, Jesus can set them free.

The church has changed so much. Some are located in communities where a lot of the afore-mentioned people live. There's no outreach. Everything is done inside. No one comes out to help the unfortunate, or the displaced. It seems as if the church has become nothing more than a social club where people, who haven't seen one another, come to meet and catch up on old times.

Let's talk about another person to whom the church should show love.

The Backslider:

When the parable of the Prodigal Son is preached, the church shouts, and praises God. There's not a dry eye in the house. When a backslider actually comes to the church and repents, asking the church to pray for him, it's a different story. Nobody wants him around. They shun him, and they talk about him, behind his back. If he joins the church, they'll do everything they can to run him off. Let's look at the Word of God, and see what he says about this.

> "What man of you, having a hundred sheep, if he loses one of them, does not leave the ninety-nine in the wilderness, and goes after that which is lost, until he finds it? And when he has found it, he lays it on his shoulders, rejoicing. And when he comes home, he calls together his friends and neighbors, saying unto them, Rejoice with me; for I have found my sheep, which was lost." (Luke 15: 4-6)

Why can't the church rejoice like that, when someone lost comes back home? If it were one of their relatives, all of them would probably rejoice. When did we lose our regard for the lost? No one seems to care anymore.

I've been a backslider. I've gone to the church for help. I was scorned and shunned. I tried to talk to the pastor. He looked at me as if I had a bad disease. He would use the scripture to preach about me, to his congregation. Afterward, everyone knew I was a backslider. They wanted nothing to do with me.

> "Brethren, if a man be overtaken in a fault, you which are spiritual, restore such a one in the spirit of meekness; lest you also be tempted." (Galatians 6:1)

The above scripture is wonderful. It would be even more wonderful, if the church complied with it. I am not saying all churches are like that. I am only speaking from experience. Each time I went to the church for restoration, I never got it. Not even an attempt was made in that direction. It makes you feel bad. It makes you feel unwanted, worthless. I mean, I am a child of God. Why wouldn't other children of God help me?

Remember The Prodigal Son parable? Well, I was the younger son, who left the father's house, repented, and came back home. I never got the party, and the good reception. I did get the attitude of the older son, who was angry because the father accepted the younger son back. I got a lot of that, and I wasn't accepted. Were these real church people?

I'm afraid a lot of churches are like the older son, in The Prodigal Son parable. He was a legalist. They think they are better than the backslider, like the older son felt he was better than his brother. He judged his backsliding brother, and thought he should be punished. The older son quickly pointed out the sins of his younger brother, but didn't forget to also point out that he had committed none. To the contrary, he committed several.

The older son thought that because he never left home, he hadn't sinned. Not so! He was guilty of self-righteousness, pride, and being slothful. He thought that by works he had pleased the father. He never put his faith to work, and faith without works is dead. He just kept following the rules, but his legalism fell short of pleasing the father.

There are so many, in the church, like that. They think that because they never went out into the world and sinned, they're better than the backslider. I guess they never realized they could sin, while still in the church. Paying tithes, taking communion, and church attendance are all things they should do. They aren't things that will get you in good standing with God. That's works, not faith. You can't please God without faith (Hebrews 11:6).

The backslider is still a child of God. He hasn't lost his salvation. He's still saved. The church needs to welcome the backslider. She needs to help restore him, and get him back into serving the Lord. When the church does that, she saves a soul from eternal damnation.

There is one more thing I must mention about love being in the church. This is paramount. Without this, there can be no love in the church. When the church loves this, it shows love is present. Check this out.

Loving The Proclamation Of Jesus Christ:

When the spirit of God is in the church, the love of God is in the church. The spirit of God and the spirit of love are synonymous. We have mentioned that before. The spirit of God proclaims and manifests Jesus Christ. Look at what the Word of God says about that.

> "Howbeit when he, the spirit of truth, is come, he
> will guide you into all truth: for he shall not speak
> of himself; but whatsoever he shall hear, that shall
> he speak: and he will show you things to come.
> He shall glorify me: for he shall receive of mine,
> and shall show it unto you. (John 16:13-15)

It's evident from the scripture above that the Spirit of God manifests Jesus Christ. Therefore, the name of Jesus, the life of Jesus, the death of Jesus, the resurrection of Jesus, and the second coming of Jesus should be proclaimed.

Watch out for those churches that worship a spirit, but Jesus is never mentioned. I have been to some like that. They worship a spirit and they call him god. But when there's a spirit, and that spirit doesn't manifest Jesus, that spirit is a contrary spirit. It isn't of God. That isn't the spirit of love. That's a spirit of bondage, and everyone filled with it is enslaved. One of the practices of those churches is they lay hands on you when they pray for you. That's how they transfer spirits into your body.

Prayer is communication with God. Laying hands on another person doesn't mean God has heard your prayer. You pray from your heart, through your mouth. Touching the person you are praying for, or the person you are praying with, is futile. God isn't listening to your hands, because hands don't speak. He hears the voice, generated from the spirit, with a sincere heart.

The scripture often used to justify that practice is Matthew 18:19, which says, "Again I say unto you, That if two of you shall agree on earth as touching anything that they shall ask, it shall be done for them of my Father which is in heaven."

The distortion comes in when the word "touching" is referred to each other, and that is not what the text says. The scripture doesn't say we should touch each other. It says, "…touching anything that they shall ask." In other words, when two people agree (touching) on anything being prayed for, God will grant it. Then, the thing being prayed for is established by two witnesses before God. Got it? Okay! Let me get back to Loving the Proclamation of Jesus Christ, now.

In a lot of churches, Jesus is not mentioned that much. You hear the Word God, but the name of Jesus is not mentioned. If Jesus is not mentioned, the gospel is not being preached. "…for there is no other name under heaven given among men, whereby we must be saved" (Acts 4:12). Without Jesus, there's no salvation. "That if you shall confess with your mouth the Lord Jesus, and shall believe in your heart that God raised him from the dead, you shall be saved" (Rom. 10:9). If people are going to be saved, Jesus must be proclaimed.

In John 14:6, Jesus says, "I am the way, the truth, and the life; no man comes to the Father, except by me." Here's another reason why Jesus must be preached. So many people believe there's more than one way to get to God. Why won't people believe the Bible, and just take God at his word?

Jesus said, "I am the way." There are so many people looking for the way to God, and haven't found it. Why haven't they found it? They are following things and people, rather than following Jesus Christ.

In this self-willed society, no one wants to be told what to do. They feel their lives belong to them, and they know what's best. They make their own decisions, and do what they want. They do what feels good. They listen to what sounds good, and they go after what looks good. However, doing what pleases them doesn't help them find the way to God. After all that pleasure, they still remain lost.

Jesus also said, "I am the truth." He's not just logical truth, reasonable truth, existential truth, or scientific truth. He is *absolute* truth. There's no contradiction in him. He's perfect in his expression, and in his manifestation. There are no miscalculations.

That's why Jesus said, "He that has seen me, has seen the Father" (John 14:9). "For I and the Father are one" (John 10:30). "He is the image of the invisible God…" (Colossians 1:15). No one can show you God better than Jesus Christ. Follow him, and you will know God. Study the word of God, and continue to obey it. "Then, you shall know the truth, and the truth shall set you free" (John 8: 31, 32).

Jesus also said, "I am the life." It is recorded in John 1:4, "In him was life, and the life was the light of men." Remember that song the old folks used to sing? "This little light of mine, I'm gonna let it shine. Let it shine. Let it shine. Let it shine."

The above scripture says that the life of Jesus is the light of men. That's why it's so important for Jesus to be proclaimed. In a dark world, the light of righteousness must shine. It will only shine through the men who have received Jesus as Lord. "And this is the record, that God has given to us eternal life, and this life is in his Son. He that has the Son, has life; and he that has not the Son of God has not life" (I John 5: 11-12). So, let your light shine, and let others see Jesus in you.

CHAPTER 9

LOVING YOUR ENEMIES

One of the most difficult things to do is love your enemies. I know we frequently talk about it in church, but how many of us find it easy to love those who have stolen from us, slandered our names, or have lied on us? How many of us forgive those who smile in our faces, and stab us in our backs? We do try, but forgetting the offense isn't that easy, is it? Even when we say we have forgiven someone, when we see them again, the anger is resuscitated, as if the offense happened that very moment. Look at what the scripture says about this. This is Jesus talking.

> "You have heard that it has been said, you shall love your neighbor and hate your enemy. But I say unto you, Love your enemies, bless them that curse you, and do good to them that hate you, pray for them which despitefully use you; and persecute you...For if you love them which love you, what reward have you? Do not even the publicans the same? And if you salute your

131

brethren only, what do you more than others?
Do not even the publicans so?" (Matt. 5: 43-44,
46-47)

We live in a society wherein an eye for an eye is the way we
handle offences. We have to pay back, whoever wrongs us. It's a
matter of image. We don't want to appear to be a weakling, or a
pushover. If we fail to handle it, we may lose the respect of the
people we know. Our reputation would be ruined, and everyone
else will think they can do the same thing, and get away with it.
So, we set out to get revenge.

Romans 12:19 says, "Vengeance is mine. I will repay, saith
the Lord." I know. It's hard to obey that scripture when you're
angry with someone, especially if that person is someone you
considered a friend. That hurts even more. Still, God commands
us to love our enemies. We must forgive the trespasses others
commit against us.

Matthew 6:15 says, "But if you forgive not men their trespasses,
neither will your Father forgive your trespasses." I certainly don't
want God to withhold his forgiveness toward me, and my sin is
held over my head. I want a good relationship with God.

I have heard people say, 'I will never forgive you for what you
have done." That person thinks by forgiving someone, they're doing
them a favor. That's not altogether true. Forgiveness does release the
other person from the burden of guilt. However, when you forgive
someone, that forgiveness is more for you than the other person.

What do you think would happen if you didn't forgive the
other person? First of all, unforgiveness opens a door for the
devil to come in and set up a stronghold in your life. What type
of stronghold? Bitterness, vengeance, anger, distrust, suspicion,
paranoia, violence, etc. You don't want those behaviors to weigh
you down. You won't be a happy camper. Your life will be
miserable. Trust me.

Before I go on, let me tell you what forgiveness actually is. A lot of people say the words, "I forgive you." Forgiveness is much more than that. What do those words mean, if you're still holding on to the offence committed against you?

The word forgive literally means *to cast away*. It means to cast away the offence into oblivion. Does that mean you don't remember the offence? No! You may, indeed, remember the offence. What you will no longer have are the emotional feelings associated with the offence.

Suppose your best friend slept with your girlfriend? Of course, that made you angry. When you forgave him, however, that anger was cast away. Now, a year later, when you see him, that anger doesn't return. Why? You have forgiven him, and cast the anger away. You still remember the incident, but it no longer makes you angry. If it still makes you feel the same way you felt when the offence was committed, you haven't forgiven. Instead, those feelings have, now, become a grudge that may last five, ten, or even fifteen years, and the devil has constructed a stronghold in your mind. Forgive, and you and the offender will be free.

Instead of getting revenge, the above-mentioned text says to bless your enemy, and don't curse them. Blessing someone doesn't always entail giving gifts. It only means to *speak well* of someone, instead of dragging his name through the mud.

When David said, "I will bless the Lord at all times…" (Psalms 34: 1), he meant he would speak of his goodness, not his wrath, or his judgment. That's how we bless our enemies. We speak of the good things about them, not the bad things. We lift them up, not bring them down.

I used to try to avoid my enemies. I would secretly hope something bad would happen to them. The things I thought of were awful, none of which were commensurate with who I was. They were criminal, and I would go to jail, if I did them. I wasn't a gangster. What was I thinking? Anger, when it takes hold of you, does that. It makes you think evil things. It can turn you into someone you'll regret becoming. I hated myself as much as I hated my enemies. Then, I read the following scripture.

> "Blessed are you, when men shall hate you, and when they shall separate you from their company, and shall reproach you, and cast your name as evil, for the Son of man's sake. Rejoice ye in that day, and leap for joy: behold, your reward is great in heaven: for in the like manner did their fathers unto the prophets." (Luke 6: 22-23)

The scripture above says you are blessed when people hate you and separate you from their company. When God intends to use you, he places something within you that evil people can see. Often, they see it before you can see it. And they hate it, because it's different from what's inside them. The spirit inside them is of the world, whereas the spirit inside you is of God.

So, they talk about you, and spread lies about you. They don't want you in their company, because they want their deeds to be hidden from you. They know you're righteous, and they're evil. They like being evil, but they don't want you to know they're evil. So, they spread lies to discredit your reputation, in an effort to bring shame and guilt upon you. They think they look better, when they do that.

You are blessed, because God has made you different, and has a plan for you. He knows that separation hurts you, because you thought they were your friends. God had to reveal to you your difference. When he closes a door, don't get angry. That's his way of showing that you don't fit, in that environment. You can't see it at that time, and you try to hold on to something God is trying to separate you from. The pain that comes after, usually makes a person get closer to God. Sometimes, people have to learn the hard way.

I had a friend who suffered tremendous emotional trauma because he wanted what God didn't want him to have. My friend fell in love with a woman who was of the night. Her only interest was pleasure and money. My friend, ignorant to that culture, didn't know that. The woman was artful in deceit and manipulation. Needless to say, my friend was heartbroken. He never thought the woman he loved would cheat on him, with other men. He kept forgiving, and she kept cheating. He finally got the message, and discovered God had a better plan for him. It took much pain and misery for my friend to find that out. He's now the pastor of a large church, with a beautiful and faithful wife, and one daughter. When he preaches about being unequally yoked, he knows what he's talking about.

God uses your enemies to get you where he wants you to be. So many times we enter certain environments to be accepted. From a distance, certain people look like they have everything going for them, and we want to be a part of that. When we do get in, we start to drink, smoke marijuana, and commit fornication. We have to. If we don't, we aren't loyal to the group. That's when we become suspect, and are eventually ostracized from the group. Of course, reproaches and slanders are added to our names. Then, we are hated and despised by everyone, not just the group.

Enemies can make you hate them. We must do good to our enemies. It's not good to hold grudges. They just wear you down." "Be not overcome of evil, but overcome evil with good." (Romans 12:21). Often, being good to your enemy makes him hate his bad behavior, and repent.

The scripture above says we should pray for our enemies. Being able to do that takes time. That doesn't happen overnight. Let me tell you what helped me. I started to look at the destination possibilities for my enemies. I didn't want anyone to go to hell. I began to pray for them. I asked the Lord to forgive them for what they did to me, because they were lost, and didn't know what they were doing. I began to recognize that the devil had them, and they weren't aware of what they were doing. They were controlled by Satan, and there was nothing they could do. I prayed that God would destroy any strongholds in their minds.

Loving people who love you isn't that difficult. That's easy! What reward is in that, though? Even drug users do that. Prostitutes do that. Thieves even do that. Loving those who love you isn't a great achievement. How does that make you look unique? Christians ought to be unique. We should have a love that shines. It should baffle and inspire others. We don't just love other Christians. We love everybody, even our enemies.

In case you haven't noticed, the world is expressing their hatred for Christianity more and more. They don't hate Christians because Christians have done something to them. They hate the God Christians represent. If Christians were of the world, the world would love their own. Because Christians are not of the world, the world wants to eliminate the presence of God, and the knowledge of Jesus Christ. The desire is a futile one, but that doesn't stop them from trying.

We are not responsible for the actions of others. We are, however, responsible for our own. When others persecute us, we have to love them, and do good to them. Revenge is for the Lord. He says, in Romans 12:19, "...Vengeance is mine; I will repay, saith the Lord." It's useless to want revenge, or to hold a grudge. Leave it to the Lord.

People don't realize that, when they hold grudges, they judge the other person. Oh yeah! An assessment is made concerning what they did, and a conclusion is formulated about the punishment the person deserves. When we do that, we condemn ourselves. Let's look at what God's word says about that.

"Judge not, that ye be not judged. For with what judgment you judge, ye shall be judged: and with what measure ye mete, it shall be measured to you again. And why beholdest thou the mote that is in thou brother's eye, but considerest not the beam that is in thou own eye? Or how will thou say to thou brother, Let me pull out the mote out of thine eye; and behold, a beam is in thine own eye? Thou hypocrite, first cast out the beam out of thou own eye; and thou shall see clearly to cast out the mote out of thou brother's eye." (Matthew 7: 1-5)

We're not to judge our enemies. We're to forgive them. We never have enough information with which to judge someone. Not only do we have insufficient data, we're not qualified to judge others. What? You think your hurt and your anger qualifies you to judge someone? Of course, it doesn't. We're not good enough. We're just as unclean as our enemies.

The above scripture says we shouldn't judge others. If we do, God will judge us. Not only will he judge us, he'll judge us in the same manner we judged others. He'll apply the same methods we used, and also the same rules we used. Don't think that because it doesn't happen immediately, God has forgotten. God has a way of doing things at the right time. Do you realize why God judges those who judge others? When we attempt to judge others, we put ourselves in God's place. He will not allow anyone to usurp his authority.

One thing we fail to look at, when judging others, is ourselves. While we are trying to get the speck out of the enemy's eye, we ignore the fact we have a log in our own eye. That log makes us incapable of seeing clearly. The log also makes us ineligible and unqualified to judge anyone.

God calls a person like that a hypocrite. You know what a hypocrite is. That's a person who preaches one thing, but practices another. They don't follow their own principles. They want others to follow them, but they fail to follow them themselves. I told you the Pharisees were not dead.

I know you recognize them. They're the people who go all out to enforce the rules. Of course, they don't obey any of them. They feel they are better than the rules. The rules are for the people they think are beneath them. You get the picture, now? Those are the people God will judge.

The best thing we can do is to get rid of the things that are wrong with us, before we attempt to get rid of things wrong with others. If we would concentrate on that, we would see more clearly to help someone else. It really defeats the purpose, when we try to correct someone, and we're just as problematic. No wonder Jesus said to love your enemy. He was trying to keep us from condemning ourselves. Our own judgment comes back on us. Who knows? It may be more than we can handle.

I realize this statement may sound strange, but I'm thankful for my enemies. That's right! I am thankful for the people who betrayed me, slandered my name, lied on me, and stabbed me in the back. Those people helped me.

I told you before, I was a backslider. I left a loving environment to go into an environment where there was no love. I didn't fit in, but I didn't know that right away. I found out through manipulation, deception, pain, and heartache, I was in the wrong place. While I thought I was in the right place, the people there showed me who I really was. I wasn't like them.

I discovered I couldn't live by the principles of that environment. I wasn't good at deception. I wasn't good at hurting people. I couldn't brag about breaking up someone's marriage, or destroying someone's career. I couldn't brag about tricking someone out of the money they were saving for their kid in college. I was considered a trick, because I didn't have "*game.*" I didn't fit in, and I thank my enemies for making me see that.

I was involved with people who were incapable of loving anyone but themselves. They lived by covetousness and lust. The men always wanted the other man's woman, and the women always wanted the other woman's man. They traded bodies as if they were commodities at a swap shop. There was no shame, and there was no guilt.

In the environment I was in, love was a no-no. No one wanted it, and no one was giving it. It was so deceptive. The women acted as if they accepted love, but they didn't really want it. They cheated every chance they got with other men, some with other women. All they wanted was sex, not love.

Another thing my enemies did for me was cause me to go back to God. I sought his forgiveness, his presence, and his mercy. I began to pray more. I started to read his word more. I saw my mistake in backsliding. I knew where I belonged, and I sought him with all my heart.

I remember being called weak because I believed in love. I was called a fool. Well, I discovered I was not weak. Instead, I was the stronger one. I found out it takes strength to love. That's why God gives the Holy Spirit, because no one has the power to love in his own strength. It's easy to run away from something that's good for you, or from something you need. Any coward can run. That's easy! But to put in the effort to love your enemies takes strength. That takes the power of God.

I realized I wasn't the one living in fear. They were the ones who were afraid. They were hiding from love, because they knew their emotions would be exposed. So, to protect themselves, they constantly lived in a shell of pretense. I know being heartbroken is terrible, but living in a shell to escape any further heartache, has to be even more miserable.

None of us know how a relationship will turn out. It can be good, or bad. If, by chance, something should go wrong, and our hearts are broken, that's life There's always a lesson to be learned from it. That's how we become better people. David said, in Psalms 119: 67, "Before I was afflicted, I went astray: but now have I kept thou word." Trouble has a way of bringing us back to where we are supposed to be. Thank God for your enemies. Pray for them. Be good to them. You don't have to hang out with them. Just be civil.

God has a way of shaping us. He often uses suffering to burn away any unwanted characteristics we shouldn't take with us, to the place he intends to take us. Our enemies are the tools used by God to refine us by the fire of trouble.

Some of our old habits have to be eliminated, because they are hindrances to our growth. God has a plan for all of us. We can't be the same person, when we get to where he's takings us. The old person has to remain in the past. He can't go with us into the future. We can't take the old friends God eliminated from our lives either.

Suppose God is taking you to sit among kings? There are some things you must drop. That suffering caused by your enemies was all a part of God's plan. They were just doing what they were supposed to do. That's why you weren't killed. Those enemies weren't there to kill you. They were only there to help refine you.

The process of refinement is not pleasant. Sometimes, it feels as if you're going to die. At other times, it feels as if you're losing your mind. Yet, when the process is over, the finished product is exactly what the Lord wants, a vessel he can use for his glory. He uses your enemies for such a process.

You think Nelson Mandela liked being in prison for 27 years? His refinement process was a very long time. That's why we shouldn't complain about the suffering we're required to go through. God used Mandela's enemies to help in the refinement of a great servant. After Mandela was released, he forgave his enemies, and went on to become the Prime Minister of South Africa. Thank God for your enemies. God uses them for his purpose.

Remember Joseph, in the Bible? You can find his story in chapters 37-45, in the book of Genesis. His enemies were also instrumental in causing him to be exalted to greatness. His enemies were his own brothers. They hated Joseph because their father loved him more than he loved them. To show his love for Joseph, their father made a coat of many colors for Joseph. His brothers became even more furious. Even though they hated Joseph, God had a plan for Joseph's life that would bring him glory.

One night Joseph had a prophetic dream, telling him a little about God's plan for his life. In the dream, his brothers were bowing down to him, revealing that he would, one day, rule over them. When Joseph told his brothers, they threw him into a pit, and sold him to a passing caravan, on its way to Egypt. They, in turn, took Joseph's coat of many colors, spread some animal blood on it, and told their father that a wild animal had killed Joseph.

In Egypt, Joseph was sold as a slave. He fared well, until his boss' wife accused him of attempted rape. For that, he spent two years in prison. While in prison, his ability to interpret dreams got around. When the king had a prophetic dream that none of his staff could interpret, Joseph was called from prison to interpret the dream.

The nature of the dream was a warning of a famine that was forthcoming. The dream said there would be 7 years of plenty, and 7 years of famine. Joseph advised the king that, if he would store his grain during the years of plenty, there would be adequate grain during the famine. The king liked the idea, and placed Joseph over all the business of Egypt. Joseph went from being a prisoner, to second in command to the King. God used Joseph's enemies as instruments, to exalt him for his glory.

Love your enemies. God has a purpose for them. He uses them to help refine you for his glory. Thank God for your enemies. Be good to them, and give God the praise.

CHAPTER 10

LOVE AND THE WORLD

As children of God, we're in the world, but not of the world. That means we're physically in the world, but we don't live by the principles of the world. We live by the Word of God, and are led by the Spirit of God. Therefore, the love inside us is different from the love in the world. The love we have is godly. It has a godly purpose with a godly effect, both of which are different from love in the world.

The world is a hateful place. It's a selfish environment. The principles the world lives by aren't conducive to loving others. The world's slogan for life is "Every man for himself." The world lives by the flesh. The flesh doesn't care for others. It's evil, greedy, and apathetic. Listen to what the word of God says about the character traits of the world.

> "For all that is in the world, the lust of the flesh, and the lust of the eyes, and the pride of life, is not of the Father, but is of the world." (I John 2:16)

Lust Of The Flesh:

The above scripture says that the lust of the flesh is one of the world's life principles. We have discussed the flesh in an earlier chapter, but it wouldn't hurt to mention it again. When the Bible uses the word flesh, it isn't talking about the skin. The flesh refers to the sinful nature of man. Lust of the flesh entails the desires of the human nature, which are always sinful. Look at what the Word of God says about the flesh.

> "Now the works of the flesh are manifest, which are these; Adultery, fornication, uncleanness, lasciviousness, idolatry, witchcraft, hatred, variance, emulations, wrath, strife, seditions, heresies, envyings, murders, drunkenness, revellings, and such like..." (Galatians 5:19-21)

As you can see, there is nothing good in the above list. Love isn't on the list, at all. There's sexual immorality, the worship of idol gods and demonic associations in witchcraft. Divisions, cliques, hatred, fighting, and violence, are present among those who live in the flesh. Of course there's ambition, envy, back stabbing, covetousness, jealousy, and murder. There's drunkenness, parties, orgies, and unusual (kinky) pleasures. Are you able to understand Paul's suggestion, in Romans 12:2, now, when he says, "Be not conformed to this world; but be ye transformed, by the renewing of your mind, that you may prove what is that good, and acceptable, and perfect, will of God?"

The Apostle Paul was right, when he said there's no good thing in his flesh. Look at how he puts it in Romans 7:18-20.

> "I know I am rotten through and through, as far as my old sinful nature (flesh) is concerned. No

matter which way I turn, I can't make myself do right. I want to, but I can't. When I want to do good, I don't; and when I try not to do wrong, I do it anyway. Now, if I am doing what I don't want to, it is plain where the trouble is: sin still has me in its evil grasp." (LB)

Those who live by the flesh can't do what's right. Therefore, they can't love. Sin has such a hold on them, they can only do what is wrong. They want to do right, but they can't. When they try not to do wrong, they do it anyway. Evil has a grasp on them. They are solely led by their own desires. "So then they that are in the flesh cannot please God" (Romans 8:8).

The spirit that lives in the children of God is different from those who live in the world. We have the Spirit of God. That doesn't mean we don't have a sinful nature. To the contrary, we fight against the flesh daily. We "walk in the Spirit in order not to fulfill the lust of the flesh" (Galatians 5:16). It's a war! Every day, the flesh tries to influence us. One thing we've discovered is, the one you feed most becomes stronger. That's why we have to feed the spirit with the Word of God daily. Let's look at the Word of God, and see what traits the spirit of God possesses.

"But the fruit of the Spirit is love, joy, peace, longsuffering, gentleness, goodness, faith, meekness, temperance; against such there is no law." (Galatians 5:22-23)

Love is at the top of this list. There's no love in those who live in the flesh. There is, however, love in those who walk in the spirit. Unfortunately, these two spirits oppose each other. Their desires are against one another. The flesh doesn't want love, joy, peace, patience, kindness, goodness, gentleness, and self-control.

Why? Those things represent God. The flesh desires whatever it wants. It desires to please only one person—self.

Lust Of The Eyes:

Another trait of the world is lust of the eyes, which is another way of saying *greed.* The world is a greedy place. It's greedy because it covets the possessions of other people. People who live by the flesh are never satisfied. They never have enough. They always want more.

They want your wife, your job, your position, your power, and even, at times, your image. People of the world covet everything. They see something they want one day. The next day, they've changed their minds, and they want something altogether different.

What they want doesn't need to have any significance. They merely want the prerogative of saying they own it. They may keep it. They may not. People will know they own it. That satisfies them. It makes them feel important. Wasn't it Jesus who said, "Take heed, and beware of covetousness: for a man's life consisteth not in the abundance of the things which he possesseth?"

It's true. No one can take any of his possessions with him to the grave. Yet, many think those possessions make them who they are. So many people define themselves by what they do, where they live, and the money they make. After all the acquisitions, "What does it profit a man, if he shall gain the whole world, and lose his soul" (Mark 8:36)?

I look at the young millionaires, today. Come on! How many cars does one person need? And how many bedrooms does a family of one need? Who can wear that many pair of sneakers? I mean, you've been blessed by God to be extremely wealthy, and who is it helping?

What people in the world don't understand is, God didn't give you what you have just for you to showcase. No! You've been blessed to bless someone else. But when there's greed, blessing people isn't on the agenda. Instead, there's more interest in accolades, applause, and any other type of notoriety. They want to be known for their wealth. They want to be considered important. The only problem is: "If a man thinks himself to be something when he is nothing, he deceives himself" (Galatians 6:3).

Pride Of Life:

Another thing the world is known for is pride, which is a form of idolatry. There's an air of arrogance in the world. When a person is arrogant, he knows everything. He's always right, and you are always wrong. An arrogant person is very condescending. He looks down on everyone. No one ever meets his standards. An arrogant person sits on his own throne. He sits where God should be, and worships himself.

Pride presents a false existence. It causes a person to live as an imposter. What appears outside isn't what's really inside. The outside is only a projection of what a person wants others to think. The outside is usually a camouflage of the inferiority, or fear, inside. Nevertheless, people tend to boast and brag about things that are, most likely, not true.

Proverbs 18:16 says, "Pride goes before destruction, and a haughty spirit before a fall." Remember Lucifer? He was the most beautiful angel in heaven. He was in charge of praise and worship. He could open his mouth, and the sound of any instrument would emit therefrom. One day, however, he started to believe his own press. Pride sat in, and Lucifer got bigheaded. He began to worship himself.

After pride engulfed Lucifer, he began to think he should rule heaven, and not God. That's what pride will do. It makes you think you are entitled to more than you actually deserve. As a result, he influenced one-third of the angels to participate with him in an insurrection against God (Rev. 12:7-9). When cast out, he became Satan, Devil, Prince of the air, Beelzebub, thief, liar, tempter, slanderer, god of this world, and accuser of the brethren. The angels that accompanied him became demons. He, now, lives in chains of darkness.

God doesn't like pride. In James 4:6, the Word of God says, "...God resists the proud, and gives grace unto the humble." God does not give his glory to others. People with pride are idolaters. They worship themselves. Therefore, God resists them. He does not give them grace (*his unmerited favor*). He opposes them, because He says, in Exodus 20:3, "Thou shalt have no other gods before me."

So, when you see arrogance, or someone bragging without giving God credit, remember that he doesn't have the favor of God. In fact, God opposes him, because he ignores God, and places himself in the god position.

God gives grace to the humble, those who know they can do nothing without him. They recognize their dependence upon God, and praise him for his assistance. They tell of God's goodness, and of all his blessings. They take no credit for their achievements. They give God the glory, because they know he's in control of their lives.

The humble blesses God for their successes, and they praise him for their failures. Everything is of God. The achievements are his favor, because he wanted them to have them. The failures are his favor, too, because he didn't want them to have them. Both are for their good, and both are for God's glory.

The three things I've mentioned are not of the Father. They are of the world. The children of God aren't to love the world.

"…Whosever, therefore, will be a friend of the world is an enemy of God" (James 4:4). You cannot have your cake and eat it, too.

Have you ever thought about why the world hates Christians, and why they don't want them around? The Bible says they have the life of Jesus in them. That life is light that shines into darkness. Those who live in darkness hate the light, because the light shows that their deeds are evil. They don't want their deeds to be exposed, so they do everything they can to keep the light from them.

Sometimes, Christians take the response of the world personally. They shouldn't. The hatred of the world isn't directed at the person, but at the spirit inside the person. That's who they don't want. They don't want God. It is God they reject, not you. And so many Christians wonder why they don't fit in, and are not accepted. Well, now you know.

For the Christian, who is still trying to fit in with the world, and is continually rejected, the world will never love you. You are wasting your time. Christians have nothing in common with the world. Why? Light has nothing in common with darkness. Everyone knows that. Light dissipates darkness. It makes it disappear. How can the two hang out together? Darkness will only hate you, because it sees you as a threat.

The absence of love in the world is mainly because of not knowing God. "He was in the world, and the world was made by him, but the world knew him not" (John 1:10). Those who are of the world do mind the things of the world. Those who are of God mind the things of God. These two are opposite, and they oppose each other. The world hears her own. Those who are of God hear the Word of God.

When it comes to God, the world is quite pretentious. She acts as if she loves God, but in reality, she denies God. Churches are filled with those types of people. "They have a form of godliness, but they deny the power thereof" (II Timothy 3:5).

They think they have a viable relationship with God, when their church attendance is at 100% for the year. Paying the tithe and taking communion certainly indicate they are close to God. Don't forget baptism! Of course, that cinches their relationship with God. Baptism definitely makes them a child of God. After the benediction is given, however, these same people curse you out on the parking lot of the church, before they even get home. They look Christian on the outside. Inside, the love of God is missing.

There's no love in the world, because there's no God in the world. It's an evil place. You've heard the old saying: Good people finish last. That's because the world hates righteousness. People of the world like to see blood. They don't care much for kindness.

Look at whom the world celebrates—self-made celebrities. They put drug addicts, strippers, fornicators, and criminals on a pedestal, and make legends out of them. People who dedicated their lives doing good for others, are scarcely remembered. The people who lived on drugs, and killed themselves with drugs, seem to get all the notoriety. So do those who lived lives of violence, and were killed by the very violence they perpetrated. However, those who were assassinated while fighting for the rights and welfare of humanity, they seem to be forgotten. Not much value is given to their efforts. Now, look at whom God exalts.

> "For you see your calling brethren, how that not many wise men after the flesh, not many mighty, not many noble, are called: But God hath chosen the foolish things of the world to confound the Wise; and God hath chosen the weak things of the world to confound the things which are mighty; And base things of the world, and things which are despised, hath God chosen, yea, and things which are not, to bring to nought things

that are: That no flesh shall glory in his presence."
(I Corinthians. 1:26-29)

The world exalts people that display their principles. God, on the other hand, exalts those who project his principles. When God chooses whom to use for his glory, he doesn't pick the wise man after the flesh. In other words, he doesn't go to the halls of academia to choose someone gifted in the wisdom of the world. He doesn't pick the mighty, someone endowed with the power of the world. High ranking positions in society aren't important to God. He doesn't choose the affluent, because nobility doesn't impress him.

When God chooses someone for his glory, he chooses the foolish, the weak, the low-class, the despised, the hated, and the based things of this world. In other words, God chooses people, who are considered useless, worthless, unrecognized, and stupid, through which to get his glory.

Didn't he use Rahab, the prostitute, to help the spies? Didn't he use Moses the murderer and the inarticulate, to lead the Hebrew children to the promise land? Didn't he use the Apostle Paul, the persecutor, to bring the gospel to the Gentiles, and pen 13 out of 27 books of the New Testament? Didn't he use Peter, the backslider, to preach the greatest sermon ever, on the day of Pentecost, and three thousand souls were saved?

God uses the least expected, and the most unlikely, to shame the world. He shows that men don't need the wisdom of the world to be successful. All they need is God. The world has its standards, and God has his. He will not share his glory with the world, or with anyone. The wisdom of the world is foolishness with God.

Those exalted by the world don't share in the glory of God. Their short-lived glory comes from man, not through God. On the other hand, the people used by God have been talked about for over 2000 years. They shall be talked about continuously, because the endorsement of God is forever. It's through them that God gets his glory.

I'm not saying there aren't men, of the world, who have made significance contributions. Certainly, there have been. Where would we be without the telephone, the automobile, the boat, the light bulb, the airplane, shoes, clothes, various medicines, etc.? Those things may be good. Do they contribute to the growth and development of humanity, though? While they are good, they don't touch the soul, or the spirit of man. Man is not regenerated by those things.

The world is so temporal. It's so finite. Nothing lasts in the world. Everything is forever changing. Nothing stays the same. When you become familiar with one thing, a new thing evolves. They call it the new and improved.

Things are so sophisticated, and so modern. You need an education to learn how to operate some things. Everything is available at just the touch of a finger. Technology has made life easier, and more comfortable. You can achieve things now in minutes that took hours before. The question remains. Has these things contributed to the betterment of humankind? Let me cite a couple of illustrations, to make my point.

I'm not saying technology isn't good. It is! It does make life easier. I think it also cripples the mind by hindering its growth and its development.

When I was in school, we had to do math in our heads. We weren't allowed to use calculators. That was cheating. The teacher would call students to the board to solve math problems. That made us study harder. We also had to stand in front of the class and recite the time tables of the day, depending on what number the class was on, at the time. We went as far as the twelve time tables. That was always where I messed up. They were difficult.

I used to do substitute teaching, mostly middle schools. I can remember the incompetency of the seventh and eighth grade students. At this time, all students were allowed calculators. As long as the children had calculators, they were brilliant. Without the calculators, however, they couldn't solve the simplest math problems. They were trained to depend upon a device, when God had already given them a mental calculator. The human device was replaced by a machine, which restricted mental development. That problem still exists, today.

I had a friend who worked as a sanitation worker. He would jump off the garbage truck, retrieve the garbage from the curb, empty it, and place the trash can back on the curb. All of a sudden, he was replaced by an electronic arm. That's what I don't like about technology. When humans lose their jobs and are replaced by machines.

The world doesn't care about humanity. People are being trained to hate, and fight against, God. Evolution is taught in schools. Darwinism is being taught as truth, while creationism is taught as a lie. The Big Bang Theory is how everything got here, according to the world. The fact that God created the world and everything in it, is a lie, according to the wisdom of the world. And man wasn't created by God, but came from animals.

> "Let no man deceive himself. If any man among you seems to be wise in this world, let him become a fool, that he may be wise. For the wisdom of this world is foolishness with God. For it is written, he takes the wise in their own craftiness." (I Corinthians. 3:18-19)

There's nothing wrong in acquiring worldly knowledge to obtain a marketable skill for work. However, to incorporate it into your life would be disastrous. In order to fulfill your purpose in life, it takes God to do that. Only God can help you become who he designed you to be. If the knowledge acquired in college is only used to get money, and not for the glory of God, you missed the boat. The wisdom of this world is foolishness with God. Look at what the word of God says.

> "And be not conformed to this world: but be ye transformed by the renewing of your mind, that ye may prove what is that good, and acceptable, and perfect, will of God." (Romans 12:2)

It's clear, from the above scripture, that God doesn't want us to be like the world. The very first phrase instructs us not to be *conformed* to this world. The word conform means to *fashion and shape something like another*. In other words, God doesn't want us to be fashioned or shaped like the world. He wants us to look like Jesus, not the world.

When a person is fashioned or shaped like something, he looks like whatever he is fashioned after. This change is an outward change, not an inward change. It is transitory, changeable, and unstable. It causes a person to act like, talk like, live like, and have the same values as the thing conformed to. That means, when the world changes, you change, too.

Instead of conforming, we should be transforming. That's what the above-mentioned text instructs us to do. It says, "Be ye transformed, by the renewing of your mind." The word transform means "to change into another form." This change is an inward change, which affects the thinking, and the character. God wants our thinking and our character, to be different from those of the world. This transformation is not an instant one. This is a life-long metamorphosis.

This metamorphosis takes place "by the renewing of the mind." The word renewing suggests *a complete renovation*. The morals change. The willingness to follow God changes, rather than following the principles of the world. You literally become a new and different person. When people encounter you, they see the image of Christ in you. You will still be in the world, but you will no longer be of the world.

EPILOGUE

I 've written this book from two sources. The first source is what I've experienced. Those, of course, were the things I saw, felt, and did. Let's not forget the things done to me also. The other source is revelation from the Holy Spirit, who helped me understand the existential things, by uncovering the meaning of them all. I don't claim to be some type of expert on love. To the contrary, the things shown to me by the Spirit were quite difficult to take. I saw the person I refused to look at, and discovered how big of a fool I really was. I also saw the growth I experienced because of those things.

This book has been therapeutic for me. Writing it has helped me see my weakness, my failure, my ignorance, and my yearning. Like everybody else, I never knew what love was. I knew I wanted it in my life. I read the popular magazines, and looked at the popular television shows. Everyone said the same thing. No one knew what he was saying, however. Yet, I listened to them, and thought I knew what love was.

Wanting love did not make me popular. I had a bad habit of treating girls nicely, in school. It was my upbringing. Girls scared me, though. The more beautiful they were, the more afraid of them I was. Even though I was fascinated with their beauty, I never knew what to say to them. I just knew I wanted to be in their company.

Rejection:

I didn't write much about this topic. Maybe I should have, because my life started with rejection. However, before I tell you about my story, let me tell you about another story I think reveals the sting of rejection, just as well as my own.

This story was told to me by one of my closest friends, who is now gone to be with the Lord. He grew up never knowing who his father was. Whenever he asked about him, he was told he didn't need to know him, because he was no good. He always wondered. Why would his relatives want him not to know his father? To him, that didn't seem right.

He finally met his father, when he was on his deathbed. His grandmother finally decided to tell him who he was. He said, he never knew what to say to him. He couldn't call him dad, or pop. He just called him by his name. He found out his father wasn't poor. He lived comfortably. He owned the neighborhood convenience store. Behind the store sat a big house, with a Mercedes in the driveway. He wasn't broke, at all. This man had money. He wondered why he never gave his mother anything to help raise him.

He was conceived in adultery, because his father was married, when he met his mother. He also had children. He apologized for not being there. Tears were coming from his eyes. Of course, he forgave his father. He didn't hate him, but neither did he know him well enough to love him. He was hurt, but he was also sorry he never got the chance to know him.

Another thing that happened to him was physical abuse. For a long time, there was only he and his mother. Suddenly, when he was about five years old, there was a man in the house. He treated him real good, at first. He thought the man was his father. Then, his mother became pregnant with her husband's first child. That's when he was no longer wanted. His mother and her new husband were building a family, and he wasn't going to be a part of it.

His new stepfather began to physically abuse him. He would beat him for no reason. My friend said he could be asleep. His stepfather would awaken him by beating him with a belt. When he told his mother, she never believed him. He could never prove it, because his stepfather never left bruises on him. One day, the stepfather got careless, and left bruises on my friend. His mother finally believed him. She didn't respond, however, the way he thought she would.

He thought he was finally rid of that mean man. His mother believed him! She saw the bruises her husband put on her son's body. She knew, now, how he mistreated him, in her absence. He just knew she was going to make him leave. Man, was he in for a surprise!

His stepfather abused him for two years. When his mother found out, he thought she would get rid of her husband. She got rid of her son, instead. She sent him to another city, to live with his grandparents. She stayed married to that mean man, and eventually had six children by him.

That rejection really hurt. He thought his own mother didn't love him, or want him around. It took him a long time to forgive her for that. He remained angry until he was in his twenties. He and his mother had a great relationship after that. He didn't see her much, because of his stepfather, but he still loved her. His mother went through some abuse also. He knows, now, all of this was in God's plan for his life.

It's amazing how God uses things like rejection to thrust us into our destinies. My friend became a powerful preacher, after his ordeal with rejection. May he rest in peace!

Where Does Love Come From?

I looked for love in all the wrong places. Initially, I thought love was an emotional utopia you lived in, when you had a girlfriend. Love came from women. They were the ones who made you feel love, so I thought. You just had to be lucky enough to get a good one, which was very difficult to find. Finding a mean woman was easy. It seemed as if they were everywhere.

After I surmised that love came from women, I had to ascertain what it was about women that made you feel love? Of course, it had to be sex. Therefore, I pursued sex. I discovered that wasn't where I was going to find love either. Sex was too shallow. It didn't make me feel love. I did feel pleasure, but it didn't make me commit to one person. I never felt fulfilled. I found out sex only made me sin. It made me lie, cheat, deceive, betray, and manipulate women.

How was I going to find something I couldn't see, and didn't know how to recognize? I was wasting my time. I didn't know what I was looking for. I started to study about love in the scriptures. I did it myself, because the church wasn't teaching it. I've never heard love taught in church, like I've written about it in this book. Sure, many have said God is love, but that's a packed statement. I needed that statement to be unpacked. That wasn't being done in church. Had that been done, I would have learned more about God, and more about love.

How many people are looking for love and do not know that love comes only from God? How many people are looking for love, and do not know the reason they cannot find it is because love is a spirit? If the church would just teach those two truths about love, people would not embark on heartbreaking searches, looking for something they cannot find.

That's why I wrote this book. I know how it feels to look for love, and never find it. I can testify about the many disappointments. I don't want to see people disappointed. I want to see people happy in love. I know everyone isn't going to accept what I've said about where love comes from. I just want everyone to know that's not just a theory. That is the Word of God.

When I discovered love is a spirit, I knew I was looking for love in all the wrong people. I found out why I was rejected so much. The women I wanted to associate with didn't have love in them. I knew that because, they weren't born of God. They weren't saved. How can you give what you don't have? Knowing that helped me in so many ways.

When I was rejected, it made me feel useless, worthless, and unimportant. I really felt I was rejected because I was inept, as a man. I was so happy, when I discovered that isn't true. I found out there was nothing I could've done to keep those women. We didn't have compatible spirits. I had the spirit of God [love], and they didn't. That didn't make me less of a man. It just made me different.

So many men have fallen for this trick of the devil. They think they're less of a man because the woman they wanted chose someone else. I used to think that, too. Listen! You aren't less a man. We are spirits, and spirits associate with spirits compatible to themselves. Sexually immoral people will hang with people who are like them. Liars do the same thing. Self-righteous people do the same. Everybody hangs with his kind. With whom else can they get along? If someone was evil, and you were good, they chose someone else because their evil spirit, and your good spirit, weren't compatible.

When God closes a door, rejoice. That's a sign that God has something better for you. When your friends say you weren't strong enough to hold your woman, just laugh it off. It was her lost, not yours. Don't try to hold on to what God doesn't want you have.

What Does Love Look Like?

I wrote this book to erase the confusion about love. I certainly went through the same confusion. I did not know what love looked like either. Do not think that because I happen to write a book, I know everything. I became a fool, to gain just a little wisdom. God has all wisdom, and what he has given me, I share with you, in this book.

As I said before, a pretty face, and a nice pair of legs was how love looked to me. Kisses and hugs were love in action. An erroneous concept about anything can keep you blind for years. I've been there.

It's believed and accepted that love hurts. If there is no pain, there is no love. I used to believe that, too. That made me think; why must love hurt? Why do I have to inflict pain upon the one I love? I would have to go to a *school of sadism*, just to learn how to show love. That was ludicrous, to even think that.

I noticed many people follow that principle. Many women search for masters to dominate, control, and abuse them. They actually want to be enslaved. I wasn't going to accept that. That wasn't a portrait of true love. Even I knew that.

I was directed to I Corinthians 13, by an old Christian woman. She told me, "If you want to know how love looks, read the love chapter." I complied with her request, and read I Cor. 13. There was nothing in there that suggested love hurts. To the contrary, it said love was kind. Why do people not accept that?

Not only did I discover love doesn't hurt, I discovered how love looked. All of the character traits of love were delineated in that chapter. I learned how to recognize love. Those traits of love showed me how love should be given. That was an eye opener. I found out how I should be treated, and how I should treat the person I love.

Another reason I wrote this book was to help people to not miss love. Love can be right in front of you and you may not know it, because you do not know how love looks. Man, I know how that feels, to miss love. I also know how it feels to be hurt by what you think is love. I learned the hard way not to fabricate my own concept of love. God is love. Let him show you what it is. If you learn the traits of love, you will be able to recognize it when you see it.

Storge:

I once had a friend, who had a daughter at a young age. He wasn't married when he had her. His methods of taking care of her landed him in prison. The mother of the child chose not to wait for him, and terminated their relationship. When released, he didn't know where his daughter, or her mother, was. He couldn't find them, and didn't have the money to hire anybody to search for them.

It was twenty-nine years before he heard from his daughter. How she found him, he doesn't know. By then, she hated him, and blamed him for their estrangement. They started to communicate on Facebook. He thought the reunion was going great, until his daughter revealed how angry she really was. She slandered him on Facebook, saying he was an unfit father, who chose not to take care of his daughter. She said, he abandoned her, which wasn't true. Her mother kept her from him. She told his daughter false things that made her hate him. The daughter, however, refused to accept the truth about what her mother did.

I do believe these things happened to him to enlighten others. The Holy Spirit showed me the meaning of these things. We aren't a family until we have given our lives to Jesus Christ. That's why I've always felt at home in church, around other believers.

The family of God is my true family. The Spirit of my father is in the rest of my sisters and brothers. That makes us family.

His daughter is still blaming him. She only contacts him to argue, and blame him for what she thinks he did. He has tried to introduce her to Jesus. She hasn't accepted that. She refuses to forgive him. That was the greatest disappointment in his life, he says.

Eros:

I've already talked a little about this. Therefore, this discourse will be a brief one.

We all know a relationship based solely on sex won't last. We go into it hoping it will, but when reality appears, we're always disappointed. I found out the hard way that sex is deceptive. It promises fulfillment, but it cannot deliver.

I've confused sex with love before. That was disastrous. That's when you *really* play the fool. I've written this book, because many are making the same mistake. Hearts are being broken, suicides committed, dreams destroyed, and revenge is dressed in murder. When people are exploited, terrible things happen.

Sex is so popular, women are exploiting themselves. Look at the internet. You have live web cams. Then, you have the personal dating ads. Young girls are having live sex. Look at how many young girls are venturing into adult films. The list is endless.

I wrote this book to help elevate the self-esteem of women. I want women to know they can be anything they put their minds to. I want them to know they don't have to take their clothes off to be somebody. Neither do they have to exploit themselves for love or appreciation. I would like women to realize they're more than a pretty face, and a shapely body. They are creations of God, with a soul, mind, and spirit.

Phileo:

I've tried to tackle this subject because I haven't been successful in this area. I know what a true friend is. I just never had one. The people, who called themselves my friend, were very pretentious. They pretended to be something they weren't. I couldn't trust any of them. They were all liars.

Not only were my friends pretentious, they were also covetous. They were greedy, and they were selfish. They were never satisfied with what they had. They always wanted what someone else had. They were idolaters. They worshipped an image of themselves.

I never had true friends. I only had fair weather friends. When things were good, they called themselves my friend. I lost my job, and couldn't find another one for a while. When I looked up, all of my fair weather friends were gone. When I got another job, they wanted to be my friend again. Thanks, but no thanks!

I learned that the Holy Spirit is the key to true friendship. Unless God is in a person, he will not be honest. When a person is trying to follow God, they are more apt to doing the right thing. They can be trusted more than a fair weather friend.

Agape:

There's no greater love than this type of love. Everyone wants this love, but refuses to accept the truth about it. This love is godly, unconditional, perfect, and everlasting. There are no flaws in this love. This love meets all your needs. It envelopes your entire being, and transforms you into the image of Christ. Then, you look like the love that's in you.

I wrote about this because I want people to know that when you seek love, you seek God. That means that, if God isn't seen in a person, love will not be seen either. It was important for me to tell everyone that. With this information, a person can make an informed decision about being with someone. They can know when a person truly loves them. That, alone, can eliminate many disappointments.

I find it amazing that people would rather be in a relationship where God is absent. They want love, but they want it without God. That's not going to happen. There can't be love without God. There's only condemnation. Let me explain. Listen to the word of God.

> "And this is the condemnation, that light is come into the world, and men loved darkness, rather than light, because their deeds were evil. For everyone that does evil hates the light, neither comes into the light, lest their deeds be reproved. But he that does truth, cometh to the light, that his deeds may be made manifest, that they are wroth in God." (John 3:19-21)

God is love. Love is God. God is light. Love is light. When people refuse to come into the light, they do it because they don't want to relinquish the evil things they do. They don't want their evil habits exposed. Therefore, they remain in godless relationships, just to keep the sins they enjoy a secret.

Agape love has no fear. There's no shame to hide. Agape is pure, and it covers the shame. It covers the mistakes. It will never fail you. It will never leave you. It makes you want to tell everyone you're in love. You want others to know its joy. Once you have it, you'll never let go. There's no substitute for it

Love And Marriage:

I wrote this book to dispel the idea that marriage is obsolete, or that it doesn't work. I realize there aren't a lot of people rushing to get married. They've been hurt, and are a little gun shy about getting married again. Don't count me out. I've been hurt in marriage, too. The divorce hurt more. I know how it feels to have a failed marriage. I still believe in marriage, though. Why did your marriage fail? Ever thought about it?

My marriage failed because I was unequally yoked. I married the wrong person, for the wrong reasons. I won't tell you the reason, but it wasn't love. I liked the girl, but I married her because I had a hidden agenda. That was wrong! Of course, the marriage ended in divorce. I perpetrated an unjustifiable falsehood. I regret doing that. I know God has forgiven me for that, but I hate what I did. Love should be the only reason for marriage. That's the only thing that will make marriage successful.

There's nothing wrong with marriage. The institution of marriage isn't at fault, when a marriage ends in divorce. The master builder designed marriage. When God created marriage, he made no mistakes. Marriage is perfect. When we follow the guidelines God has given for marriage, we can't go wrong. When we follow our own guidelines, divorce is inevitable.

Love And The Church:

I grew up in church. I came up in a certain denomination. I won't mention the denomination. I loved church. I still love church. I served in church, but I felt I was held back. It appeared to me I was hindered from realizing my spiritual potential. I became a backslider, not because I no longer loved the church. I didn't like the system of the church.

I loved the singing, the preaching, serving in the church, and the prayers. There were just too many rules to follow. The church was too legalistic. The denomination I was in put their rules before the Holy Spirit. They followed their traditions more than the Word of God.

There's no love when there is legalism. You're in bondage. You're restricted because of the rules. You can't obey God, when there're so many rules. Whenever you follow God, legalism punishes you. I was constantly punished, and eventually denied the opportunity to serve. This didn't only happen to me. I have seen preachers blacklisted and blackballed by other preachers, who think they don't have the right to preach. I think I told you, in an earlier chapter, the Pharisees aren't dead. They're still alive, in the church.

I'm not recommending you backslide whenever you dislike something in the church. I shouldn't have done so. I should have stayed to see what the end would be. Still, God did let me see something to write about. Maybe that's why God allowed those things to happen to me. He uses us all in different ways.

When I repented from backsliding, I had difficulty being accepted in church. The Bible says the church is to be instrumental in the restoration of the backslider (Galatians 6:1). Well, the churches I visited treated me with disdain. They let me know they didn't want me there. I've never felt such hatred. They acted as if I had personally done something to them. There was no love.

I want people to know that the same rule about love, that applies to people, applies to the church. If God isn't in it, love isn't present. That doesn't depend upon how well the choir sings, or how big and beautiful the building is. The Holy Spirit has to be in the church, in order for love to be present.

How can a church represent Jesus, when there's no love there? It's impossible! That's similar to a fig tree having leaves on it, but no figs. It looks full of fruit on the outside, but I's only an illusion. So many churches are like that, today. They look prosperous, fruitful, and progressive on the outside. When you get inside, however, there's nothing that resembles love. There are no ministries geared toward helping the poor, and the needy. Shouting is there, good music is there, finances are there, and popularity is there. Without the Holy Spirit, there's only emptiness. Who wants to attend an empty church?

A person can be big, even when he eats just sweets and junk food. That doesn't mean he's healthy, because of his size. When a church is big, beautiful, with a lot of members, people think that's a good church to join. That church may be big, but that doesn't mean it's healthy.

A junk food eater has a body that cannot go the distance. It has no endurance. It has no real strength. It looks strong, but it's weak. The food it eats doesn't possess the nutrients needed to create strength and endurance. A church is the same way.

When a church only serves music, and pumped-up praise, it's a weak church. Just give me the Word of God, and the Holy Spirit. If the Word is preached, taught, and the Spirit is present, love will be in the church. Lives will change, and God will be glorified.

I must caution you. When looking for a church, beware of those that have become covens for demons. The devil has infiltrated them. They look like churches that represent Jesus, but they are churches that practice witchcraft.

The devil can transform himself into an angel of light. That light is a false light. It just looks like the real light. He puts his own minster in the pulpit, which uses the Word of God to deceive you. The devil can preach the word, too. When they lay hands on you, however, demonic spirits are transferred into your body. That's how thousands become enslaved to demon spirits. They think they have God in them. In reality, they have the enemy of God, the devil, in them.

Loving Your Enemies:

I used to have a spirit of vengeance. I wanted to repay everyone that ever did me wrong. I wanted them to hurt just as much as I did. I wanted them to experience the other side of the coin. They needed to see how it felt to hurt, to be humiliated,

Then, I thought, how can I judge others when I do not have the facts, with which to make such a judgment? I do not have the ability to view the heart of man. Neither can I discern man's intentions. I am also incapable of hearing thoughts from a distance.

Am I the proprietor of man's soul? My judgment has no validity, and carries no weight. I, a mere man, do not have the power to sentence man's soul to heaven or hell. Neither place is under my jurisdiction, but is in the control of him, on whom I am dependent also. How can I judge someone, when I have no control of the future, and can't determine the destiny of others?

I've learned that enemies have a job to do. They are tools of the Lord to make you strong. God uses our enemies to refine us. The trouble our enemies bring is the fire of reshaping. It's used by God to correct and transform us into who he wants us to be. I know it's difficult to accept that. Trouble is usually painful. It doesn't feel good. The result of it, however, is a harvest of righteousness. Don't do evil for evil. Overcome evil with good.

Now, I pray for my enemies. I ask God to forgive them. I realize they don't know what they are doing, or what the consequences of their actions will be. They have no idea they are accountable to someone. They think they are invincible, and can do whatever they want. I feel sorry for them. They think they have rendered justice, when they hurt somebody. In reality, they have condemned themselves. That's why I pray for them.

Love And The World:

The world hates me. If you're a believer, it hates you, too. People of the world don't have to know you to hate you. Neither is it necessary for you to have done anything wrong. Their hared begins when they discover you believe in Jesus.

People always say, "Good guys finish last." Good guys don't finish last. People reject them because of the Christ that lives in them. In reality, people aren't rejecting them. They're rejecting God.

I had a girlfriend once, who left me for another guy. I was crushed, because I really cared for her. When she left, she told me, "I'm not really an evil person, but that's what I've become." Then she said, "I'm in another world, and you don't fit in my world. This is no place for good people."

At the time, I felt inferior. I thought the other guy was more man than me. I found out later, that's not true. I wasn't the spirit she wanted to be associated with. She didn't reject me. She rejected the Christ in me. She wanted the world.

If you are a believer, don't be surprised if the world hates you. There's no love in the world. The world hates God, and everything related to him. Stay with God, and he'll keep you in his care. No harm will come to you, as long as you stay with God.

The world will slander your name, persecute you, and make false accusations against you. It will do all it can to discredit you. It will attempt to destroy your witnessing power. Don't be surprised at who it will use against you. It may be your own children, your spouse, or the people you thought were friends.

I've seen the devil use medical doctors and nurses in attempt to destroy, or kill, one of God's children. I've seen teachers used to destroy students who believe in Jesus Christ. Judges, lawyers, and police officers are also on the devil's team. The devil will use anyone he can to steal, kill, or destroy anyone.

The world will go deeply into your past, and dig up stuff it thinks will discredit you. It will dig up stuff you were ashamed of, things you regretted. Be strong! When God is for you, he is more than the world against you.

I believe this book is enlightening, informing, and inspiring. I don't claim to be a prolific writer. I know I'm not that. Neither do I claim to know everything. This book isn't good because of me. It's good because of God.

Bye-bye. Take care. Keep loving, even when it's not reciprocated. Remember! Love is always victorious! May God continue to bless you, and keep you. I love you all.